'This is a thought-provoking, compelling, highly prac
inevitable and potentially powerful interdepend(
their communities. Using rich examples of conte
theoretical frameworks, it shows how practical chal
how we can better achieve, not only the test scor
but also the more humanly fulfilling educationai ᴗᴜᴛᴄᴏᴍᴇꜱ ᴡᴇ ᴀʟʟ ᴅᴇꜱɪʀᴇ.

Just as importantly, it reminds us that motives matter. Commitment to the
common good, to public value, enables us to achieve what other leadership
approaches cannot. Lastly, and for this reader most importantly of all, it names
both the tyranny and the poverty of measurement and invites our engagement
in the development of more honest, if more challenging, alternatives. A
timely, intelligent book rooted in reality, creating a better future now.'

Professor Michael Fielding, Institute of Education, University of London`

'There is nothing new in the idea that successful schools connect to the communities
they serve. And yet in the mad race to improve test scores this key principle
has somehow been forgotten. Drawing on the experiences of ten pioneering
schools, the authors of School Leadership for Public Value provide a challenging
and timely reminder of the importance of looking beyond the school gate.'

Professor Mel Ainscow, University of Manchester

'Mongon and Leadbeater use a broad and ambitious canvas for this thought
provoking study of school leadership and innovation. Ranging across national
and international research, they look at trends in school leadership through the
prism of "Public Value" or PV. They use the construct of PV and some associated
methodologies to measure the progress of innovation in school leadership. They
present a compelling argument that successful school leaders are reconciling a drive
for better and better teaching and learning within schools, with a recognition of the
importance and impact of a connection with the communities they draw from.

The authors provide interesting case studies to argue that recognising and
working with social context, including deprivation, does not equate to using it
as an excuse for poor attainment. They present a moral imperative for innovation
and equity, for the need to devise more engaging ways of learning for those from
the most deprived backgrounds to close the attainment gap, but to do so while
also engaging with the communities those children and their parents come from.

The authors' assertion that "the process of creating new combinations to meet new
challenges lies at the heart of most innovation" is certainly borne out by this interesting
and well written book. In an era of greater and greater autonomy for schools, and more
diffuse accountability for their success, Mongon and Leadbeater set a challenge for school
leaders and policy makers everywhere to marry their innovation to their communities.'

**Matt Dunkley, Director of Children's Services, East Sussex County Council, and
President of the Association of Directors of Children's Services (ADCS) 2011/12**

'Mongon and Leadbeater have written the right book at the right time. 21st Century learning for achievement and wellbeing requires school leadership in the service of public value. This book transcends the old divides. It correctly positions the emerging learning system as one which places communities at the centre and partnerships as the driving force. It strikes the correct balance between autonomy and accountability and casts leadership as collaborative and genuinely shared. It goes beyond the school as institution to encompass new players critical to the success of the learning game. For Mongon and Leadbeater Public Value Schools are engaged in the serious game of improvement, innovation and ultimately transformation - to ensure that all young people experience and realise the global twin goals of excellence and equity in learning.'

Anthony MacKay, Chair, The Innovation Unit Ltd, UK. Executive Director, Centre for Strategic Education, Australia

'At a time when the dominant leadership behaviours in schools tend towards being more managerial and controlling, Mongon and Leadbeater present a refreshing and well argued case for an alternative approach which promotes an authorising climate for innovation and public value. The book will provide great solace for those school leaders who are seeking evidence to challenge the accepted modus operandi by encouraging them to give up power and see their schools becoming fully engaged with their local community. Through the fantastic concept of "disruptive innovation" schools leaders are to be encouraged to develop new capacities for themselves, their staff and students and for the locality and other providers through associate leadership.

As a policy maker and school system leader I was thrilled to see such a coherent argument for a different model of practice unfold before me. As someone who seeks to authorise and promote innovation I have been limited in my endeavours by the paucity of powerful texts which support such practice. At long last a relatively brief, and very readable book, captures the essence of an alternative to the natural inclination towards control which so besets politicians and system leaders and in so doing promote a policy framework which in itself can be transformative.

Never has it been more important to consider how we can release the enormous social capital which exists in our communities - and particularly the unique role which schools can play in releasing that benefit. Mongon and Leadbeater set out how school leaders, through promoting a culture of innovation which put public value at the very heart of the system - as opposed to being at the margins - are such key figures in enabling our society to fulfil that aspiration.

The text will be of value to leaders at all levels in the education and policy environment - not just as a one off read - but as a manual for change.'

Don Ledingham, Executive Director of Education and Children's Services, East Lothian Council and Director of Education and Children's Services, Midlothian Council

School Leadership for Public Value

School Leadership for Public Value

Understanding valuable outcomes for children, families and communities

Denis Mongon and Charles Leadbeater

Institute of Education, University of London

First published in 2012 by the Institute of Education,
University of London, 20 Bedford Way, London WC1H 0AL

www.ioe.ac.uk/publications

British Library Cataloguing in Publication Data:
A catalogue record for this publication is available from the
British Library

ISBN 978 0 85473 919 6

The opinions expressed in this publication are those of the
authors and do not necessarily reflect the views of the Institute
of Education, University of London.

Typeset by Quadrant Infotech (India) Pvt Ltd
Printed by CPI Group (UK) Ltd, Croydon, CR0 4YY

Contents

Acknowledgements

We are very grateful to the leaders and other staff from the schools listed below who shared their time, expertise and wisdom generously:

- Brixham Community College, Devon
- Castle Children's Centre and Nursery School, Wakefield
- Clifton Green Primary School, York
- Coleshill Heath Primary School, Solihull
- Delaware Community Primary School, Cornwall
- Garforth Community College, Leeds
- George Green's School, Tower Hamlets
- St Thomas's Centre Pupil Referral Unit, Blackburn
- Swanlea Secondary School, Tower Hamlets
- The Westwood School, Coventry

We also need to thank Maxine Froggatt and Non Worrall who did so much during the enquiry stage to help the school leaders draw out the stories from their colleagues, pupils and parents. Barbara Spender's care and attention to the grammar and rhythms of our writing was priceless. Even then, we might not have got to publication without the encouragement of Denis's colleagues at the Institute of Education's London Centre for Leadership in Learning.

The enquiry, which drew together the schools, researchers and ourselves, was financially sponsored and in many other ways supported by the National College for School Leadership. We are especially grateful to Mark Wright, Gill Ireson, Andy Coleman and Toby Greany who, in their different roles at the College, enhanced the enquiry in a variety of ways. We are grateful to the College and to the schools for allowing us to use the information and insights which the enquiry unearthed.

The authors and publisher gratefully acknowledge the permission granted to reproduce copyright material in this book.

Figure 2.1 based on Moore, M.H. (1995) *Creating Public Value Strategic Management in Government*. Cambridge, MA: Harvard University Press. Used by permission.

Table 4.1 based on Mongon and Chapman (2012) *High Leverage Leadership: Improving Outcomes in Educational Settings.* London: Routledge, Table 2.1. Used by permission.

Table 4.2 based on Denhardt and Denhardt (2000) 'The New Public Service: Serving Rather than Steering'. *Public Administration Review*, 60:6, 554. Used by permission.

Figure 4.3 from Payne, M. and Shand, R. (2009), adapted from Payne, C. and Scott, T. (1982), *Developing Supervision of Teams in Field and Residential Social Work.* London: National Institute of Social Work, Paper No. 12. Reprinted with permission from R.C. Shand.

Every effort has been made to trace copyright holders and to obtain their permission for the use of copyrighted material. The publisher apologises for any errors or omissions in the above list and would be grateful for notification of any corrections that should be incorporated in future reprints or editions of this book.

About the authors

Denis Mongon began his career teaching in an inner London comprehensive and developed an interest in young people 'at the margins'. He was later head of a special, 'ebd', school and then Director of Hackney's Educational Guidance Centre before joining the Inner London inspectorate service and being seconded to the 1984 review of the ILEA's special education provision. For most of the 1990s, Denis was a senior officer in Hertfordshire holding briefs at different times for special needs and school improvement. His secondment in 1997 to the Chief Executive's 'Whole Organisation Review' across all the Council's services concluded with the then novel proposal to integrate Education and Children's Social Services. In 1998, he began three years at Cambridge University as 'Lecturer in Inclusion', continuing a career-long interest in enquiry which led to qualifications from London, Oxford and South Bank Universities. He is now a Visiting Professor at the Institute of Education, University of London, a Senior Research Fellow in the Education Department at Manchester University and a Senior Associate at the Innovation Unit. He has worked and written for the National College for School Leadership, including on its programmes for Directors of Children's Services. His freelance work since 2001 has included senior local government roles focused on the development of education and other children's services. He has worked with a wide range of national agencies in England, for UNICEF in Turkish prisons and for the British Council in Malawi's schools. He has also worked on system reform with national and local government in Scotland. His recently published work has described 'high leverage' school leadership raising outcomes against the odds, schools which go 'the extra mile', newly emerging models of school leadership, co-location of extended services, schools with good Ofsted grades for community cohesion and leadership which 'closes the gaps'.

Charles Leadbeater is author of a string of books on innovation in education, most recently *Innovation in Education: Lessons from Pioneers Around the World*, published by Bloomsbury in 2012, based on the work of 16 high-impact innovators in education. This followed his report and related TED talk, 'Learning from the Extremes', looking at the work of social entrepreneurs promoting new approaches to learning in the poorest parts of the developing world. Charlie is a long-time collaborator with the Innovation Unit. His 2004 report, 'Personalisation through Participation', helped to kick-start the debate over personalised learning. He followed that up with 'The Shape of Things to Come, 21 Ideas for 21st Century Learning'.

Introduction

This piece draws deeply on the work of ten schools and centres which were involved in an enquiry sponsored by the National College for School Leadership between 2008 and 2010. Our thoughts about the five tasks to which we refer in Chapter 5 began to form in a report of the early stages of the enquiry published by the National College (Leadbeater and Mongon, 2008). The work of those schools, and similar work in many others, manages to be both traditional and innovative. It stands in a long tradition of connection between schools and their local communities, stretching back at least into the nineteenth century. It is innovative because it is trying to find new ways of making those connections, and making them successful, in circumstances which do not always encourage that approach. These schools enhance outcomes for pupils by drawing on resources from within the local community and reaching out to immediate social networks and families. They also create benefits in the community (not least 'social capital') by investing their resources in the community, and encouraging the community to use these resources. The National College was interested in how these schools worked and invited them to come together and share their experiences with one another. The College provided facilitation and processes, including an online 'wiki' site, so that the learning from the group could be captured and distributed. We were asked to contribute to some of those processes and to write about the outputs. Our writing now becomes one of the outputs from the enquiry; your reading becomes one of its outcomes.

At the start of the enquiry the phrase 'public value' was borrowed from a wider discussion about public services (Moore, 1995) to summarise what the ten schools appeared to be doing. John Benington has more recently developed the concept as a lens for reflecting on the work of public services (Benington, 2009). Benington defines public value as either or both of:

- what the public values
- what adds value to the public sphere.

He points out that both of these are contested ideas in their own right and might, additionally, be in conflict with one another. There is not a consensus about 'what the public values', or whether that is what it needs or wants. However, services which consciously search for what the public values will be different in process and product from those which historically felt that the professional producer should determine a service's characteristics on the basis of superior position. Similarly, 'value added to the public sphere' is an imprecise theme, although a service which is sensitive to that will be different to one which focuses on the individual interest of current users. The sensitised service is more likely to adopt social and longer-term perspectives on the consequences of its work.

Public value was a useful concept to introduce into the enquiry because it created a framework for reflecting not just on the core activity and success of the schools – high quality teaching and learning delivering good or outstanding attainment – but also on how they worked with their partners to support that core activity in ways which generated other valuable outcomes. In broad terms, we wanted to find out whether these schools, while they provided wonderful schooling according to traditional measures, also created something akin to the four values which Benington puts at the heart of public value:

- Ecological value – actively promoting sustainable development.
- Political value – stimulating and supporting democratic dialogue, active public participation and citizen engagement.
- Economic value – generating economic activity and employment.
- Social and cultural value – contributing to social capital, social cohesion, social relationships and cultural identity as well as to individual and community well-being.

(summarised from Benington, 2009: 237)

Public Value was not a phrase with which these school leaders – or most others we expect – were familiar. Few, if any, school leaders will spend time over breakfast wondering how they might create more Public Value later in the day: they worry about the progress and well-being of both the adults and children in whose lives they carry some responsibility. This in part reflects a personal background and interest in the core business of every school – teaching and learning – and also the highly controlled accountability environment of English schools and other public services. That is an environment in which managers may be unwilling or unable to respond with leadership which seeks out public value (Wallis and Gregory, 2009: 268). Even so, because education is a key element in the wider discourse about public services, when questions are asked about the value of services to the public, education is one of the key factors which questioners and respondents are likely to have in mind. It is important that anyone with an interest in public education services can provide answers not just for the public's satisfaction but also for their own.

Three propositions about Public Value might be of particular interest in educational settings.

- When citizens believe that public services are creating value, they are more likely to support them actively as well as passively. Active engagement is more easily translated into co-production which becomes simultaneously and iteratively both an input and an outcome for the service. Taking education as an example, Talbot suggests that when parents send their children to school, higher educational attainment is not the only consequence:

  The greater parents' trust and sense of legitimacy about a school's activities, the more they are likely to contribute. So trust and legitimacy in schools is both an input to and result for these types of public agencies.

  (Talbot, 2009: 9)

- Citizens are more likely to perceive value in a service when the gap between them and its provision or reception is reduced. This is illustrated for the education service in the finding that while 80 per cent of local secondary school users were very or fairly satisfied with their service, only 30 per cent of the general population shared this view (Blaug *et al.*, 2006: 28).

- Public Value is capable of being a self-regulating and self-sustaining element in public services. Discussions about it should therefore seek to capture and to compare outputs and outcomes:

  School outputs include exam passes. School outcomes may include behaviour over a lifetime, common attitudes and 'civility', even movements in aggregate labour force productivity.

  (Walker, 2009: 5)

Of course, education is not the only public service in which co-operation between the public and the providers has enormous potential for reciprocity and a virtuous circle of increasing value: health, social services and the police would figure highly on that scale. There is an argument that across these services the term Public Value has been manipulated to suit the aims of self-serving bureaucracies which lack substantive evidence of impact and are unable to justify their existence otherwise (Alford and O'Flynn, 2009). That has been neatly summarised as follows: '*Public value: who could possibly be against it? As an objective for public service modernisation, it gives motherhood and apple pie a good run for their money*' (Crabtree, 2004).

That is far from the truth about the schools involved in the National College sponsored enquiry, for whom reality far outweighed rhetoric and accountability left no space for self-serving nonchalance. These were schools committed to the formalities of well-earned attainment and also to other less celebrated though hard-earned outcomes for their students and communities. In the context of those settings our proposal is that:

- Public value was developed when these settings provided educational services and at the same time created social outcomes that were also valued.
- Public value was created when these settings worked to improve the wider range of outcomes for their young people by engaging with families and communities in places and processes characterised by equal esteem and equitable authority.

The following pages report our enquiry, with the schools, into how public value is created by their work, the leadership qualities demanded by that work and how they judge its impact. For brevity, we have referred to the schools and centres collectively as 'the PV schools' and to their leaders as 'the PV leaders'. We hope that is not patronising.

Overview

Chapter 1: Prologue describes the national and international context for the ground-breaking work that these ten schools and centres have shared. In a fast changing economic and technological environment, international organisations, multi-national conglomerates, nation states, communities and families are all investing enormous hope in the potential of education. In its most successful and optimistic manifestations, the education of children and young people can be radical in its own right, promote economic well-being, contribute to scientific and technical understanding, nurture community cohesion and enhance family life. However, nationally and internationally, the outcomes for young people in the poorest sections of society remain obstinately low – though not consistently so within individual countries nor across countries or regions. The emergent challenge is to discover how the performances of young people, teachers, schools and communities in the weakest contexts can be brought closer to parity with the best. This section concludes by making the case for innovation and the enhancement of public value to be essential parts of the solution.

Chapter 2: Work in progress sets a wider context for change and innovation in England's public education service and introduces two tools of international provenance with which the service can be reviewed. The first of those is The Education Innovation Grid which is adapted from an international study of radical educational projects (Leadbeater and Wong, 2010). The Grid illustrates the proposal that innovation can be technical (in which case it improves or supplements current provision) or disruptive (in which case it reinvents or transforms provision). The second tool, a Public Innovation Triangle, is based on Mark Moore's public service concept (1995) and proposes that innovation requires new authorisation (disrupted governance), new capacity (disrupted resource allocation) and new measures of value (disrupted accountability mechanisms). Our proposal is that the PV schools are a cameo of that much bigger picture and are contributing disruptive innovation into the challenging triangle of capacity, accountability and measurement. The three elements of the Triangle provide the framework for considering the public value work of the schools in the National College's enquiry.

Chapter 3: A 'new story' for education? describes how what appears to be a new story for schools is based on a long history of engagement with community which has become an unacknowledged and, for some providers and policy makers, an unknown, even unwelcome, feature of the educational landscape. Chapter 3 shows how the story the PV schools have to tell contrasts with the increasing nationalisation and centralisation of the authorising environments, capacity and measures of value in the English system. National policy has emphasised a school leadership model built around strong leadership teams and the tight internal management of teaching and learning to maximise scores at the end of Key Stages. In comparison, the narrative from the PV schools emphasises the position of the school and its leaders at the heart of a school community, which is itself at the heart of other neighbourhood and professional communities. This is school leadership which knows that there is a reciprocal relationship between social, environmental and economic outcomes and the key output from schooling of student attainment. It is leadership which can acknowledge its own value without diminishing the value of other contributors – in or out of school.

Chapter 4: New authorisation records how the PV leaders develop or manipulate the authorising environments for their work and so promote a climate for innovation and the creation of public value. Central to this chapter are two proposals. The first is that authorisation can be asymmetric or associate, by which we mean in broad terms that it can be externally imposed or locally cultivated. The second is that each leader, and to some degree every individual, operates in five authorising environments defined, again in broad terms, by their personal ethics, then by association with their colleagues and students, thirdly by their governing body, fourthly by the context of neighbourhood and service communities with which they cooperate and finally by national policy makers. The chapter endorses the power of associate authorisation driven by personal ethics, working relationships and the contextual power of partnerships.

Chapter 5: Building new capacity records how the PV leaders develop new capacity for themselves, for their staff and students, for the locality and for other providers. Central to this chapter is the proposal that, in order to create new capacity, the PV leaders are engaged in five key tasks: improving the core of teaching and learning; drawing on community capacity; reaching out to generate community capacity; investing to create community capital and speculating to sponsor community capital. Their leadership must also become less managerial and controlling the further they move from work in which their position brings its own automatic authority and power. A school which limits itself exclusively to the development of its own teaching can get by with a very twentieth-century model for its leadership, management and governance – a headteacher, senior leadership team and a board of nominated governors all responsible for a single institution with a narrow purpose and a specific performance indicator for attainment at the end of each Key Stage. That model will not fit the complex demands of the work and the learning which the PV leaders were attempting when they placed themselves in circumstances where they could not rely on the formal aspects of their role. As they became involved with people and organisations outside their institution, traditional lines of responsibility and accountability became blurred and tangled. They were not always the apex of statutory authority in the room and sometimes were not even seen as a source of moral authority by some players. They had to test unexplored aspects of their personal approaches to leadership. New approaches to oversight and governance had to be considered. Since PV leaders tend to move their schools towards what might be called associate leadership (Mongon and Chapman, 2012) this comes more comfortably to them than it might to others.

Chapter 6: Measuring for value looks at how choosing the right indicators by which to measure innovation and public value is critical. It became increasingly difficult for PV schools to identify the best gauge for measuring outcomes as their work moved further away from the core of teaching and learning and its dominant measurements of attainment. Whether a young person has a C grade pass in Maths GCSE is a matter of fact. Whether their self-esteem or well-being have improved is more difficult to demonstrate and whether the improvement can be attributed to a community initiative is more difficult still. New and appropriate measures of success had to be explored without diminishing statutorily reported and, for the students, critical attainment.

Chapter 7: Conclusion proposes that the public value enquiry and others like it demonstrate what it is possible to achieve in localities and at the margins of the system. We reflect on how dependent innovation is on people who operate at the edges of the dominant structural and cultural designs. We have so much further to go if we want to fulfil the potential of that tangential thinking systemically. We propose that progress needs to be made on four fronts: developing new capacity, creating an 'authorising environment', identifying the appropriate value measures, and introducing a suitable policy framework. We suggest that local initiatives are helping to make good progress on the first two fronts though nationally we have made disappointing progress on the latter two. The public value enquiry hints at what some of the new measures might be and the success of the schools is an invitation for policy makers to take interest.

Chapter 1

Prologue

Improving educational outcomes for all

The challenges faced by the ten schools which contributed to the research reported later in this book are internationally recognisable:

- *requirements to drive standards of students' attainment ever higher;*
- *pressure to compete against other schools to secure more students and acquire additional funding;*
- *tight accountability for the achievement of narrow targets, with dire consequences for failure;*
- *deep divisions between those students who could flourish in schools and those who could not and*
- *the apparent impossibility of equalising outcomes between these two groups.*

(Ainscow *et al.*, 2012: 5)

The school leaders we worked with appeared unwilling simply to collude with a policy climate which, they believed, did not do justice to their children and families. Nor were they content to stick with recipes for teaching and learning which they knew were alienating too many families. Driven by a mixture of ambition and frustration, they had been determined to find innovative ways for their schools to meet the demands of the policy climate while providing the services and creating the engagement with their wider communities which would improve educational outcomes for all.

The economic gains to a society from improved educational performance that builds human capital and cognitive skills are impressively high. A recent Organisation for Economic Co-operation and Development study (OECD, 2010a) found that if all developed countries matched the recent improvements in Polish educational outcomes, and boosted their average scores in the Programme for International Student Assessment (PISA) by 25 points over 20 years, the economies of the OECD would grow by an additional $115 trillion over the lifetime of the generation born in 2010 (ibid.: 24). If all OECD countries managed to match the performance of the average results achieved in Finland, far and away the best performer, then the gains would be in the order of $260 trillion (ibid.). The gains from investing in better education outcomes could outweigh or counterbalance even the ups and downs of the current economic cycle. In the long run investments in effective education pay an economic dividend: good schooling underpins economic growth, higher productivity and incomes (Miller, 2008; Maddison, 2001).

The economy though is not the only area of public life which benefits from a better educated population. There is *'striking evidence of the social benefits'* accruing from extended educational opportunities (Bynner and Egerton, 2000: 44). An economist might have guessed that education would be a positive factor in a happiness equation – because increased schooling might act as a proxy for increased earnings – but there are strong indications that extended education plays a role in happiness independently of income (Blanchflower and Oswald, 2000: 11). More broadly still, '... *education is part of the socialisation process: its function in transmitting attitudes and values...,* *is a critical part of fostering shared attitudes, thus strengthening social cohesion'* (Barr, undated).

An OECD report on its five year long analytical research project has recently confirmed how strong this connection is (OECD, 2010b). That report confirmed the large body of research literature indicating that education is positively associated with a range of social outcomes including better health, stronger civic and social engagement and reduced crime (p.11). Education, it concludes, is a particularly cost effective way of improving health and reducing crime. Raising social and emotional skills appears to enable people to mobilise available information and cognitive capacity so they can better contribute to their own health and social context. Education apparently tends to have a positive direct impact on the development of those core skills and also on the *'habits, norms and ethos of healthy lifestyles and active citizenship'* (p.4). Across 27 OECD countries, citizens with 'upper secondary' or higher educational experience consistently reported better health and social outcomes than those with less than upper secondary experience (OECD, 2010c). Good schools count for a lot, if not for everything. If we can get more children for longer into better schools, with better teachers, then outcomes, measured by the kinds of tests the OECD administers, will improve.

Reforms to extend educational experience, to raise attainment and to improve wider outcomes are fraught with difficulty. They take time, money, political will, patience and determination. Children learn in a complex matrix of environments including their schools, and, no less importantly, their peer groups, families and communities. Central governments can play an indispensable role by providing a degree of consistency and coherence in their policy across those environments. However, even outside democracies, governments do not and arguably should not have the kind of grip on the learning and development of young people which would be analogous to the standard operating procedures which drive the success of some retailers, armed services and air traffic control. The danger in the potentially vital state role of sponsoring social coherence and effective pedagogy across regions and localities is that the centre's drive for consistency becomes, even after initial successes, a recipe for disciplined mediocrity. To avoid that, a society seeking to improve educational outcomes needs a steady flow of social innovations pointing towards new ways to make learning more effective and, perhaps especially, to reduce marked educational underperformance. In that context, the education service in England faces two considerable challenges if, as most would expect it to do, it seeks to improve performance and reduce inequity.

The challenges in England

First, and as we will show in more detail later (Chapter 3), the system has been increasingly subject to centralised determination of both structure and content. In pursuit of consistency, the spaces left for local innovation were purposely reduced to a minimum during the final years of the twentieth century. This led to the paradoxical introduction in 2002 of legislation to provide the 'power to innovate'. The Secretary of State may now, as a result, temporarily suspend or modify education legislation that may be inhibiting innovative approaches to raising standards. Schools, local authorities and other groups may therefore make a proposal to test innovative ideas. By 2010, across the 24,000 or so schools in England, a total of 32 innovations requiring legislative amendment had been approved, averaging four each year (DfE, 2010a). These small numbers of certificated projects hardly speak of a vibrant systemic commitment to problem solving by innovation. Fortunately, that does not reflect the whole picture. Although many schools believe that recent legislative cloth has been cut to tailor a straitjacket, others, as we will report in later chapters, continually squirm to find the pockets they can enlarge and utilise for local idiosyncrasy. Radical innovators, we are fond of saying, will always appear bonkers to most of their peers – the trick for systemic leaders is not to approve all innovation but to distinguish practical innovators from the truly bonkers and let the former get on with it.

The second major challenge for the system in England comes from the ingrained educational inequality which is written into the culture, outlook and resources of some schools and some communities. These are schools where the despondency of recurring low attainment has become habitual – sometimes for staff and students alike; these are communities that have often been left behind by economic growth, new technologies and the national shift from primary or secondary industries to service jobs. The plateau in attainment is due in large part to ingrained low engagement and the constant setbacks to aspiration for education in some communities. The links between deprivation and educational attainment are complex and the graphs which compare the academic performance of schools with the socio-economic status of their pupils are not linear. Some schools transcend the challenges they face: they buck the trend and produce student outcomes well above the average of comparable schools. Her Majesty's Chief Inspector has reported that, *'a small number of schools demonstrate that it is possible to overcome challenging circumstances and are outstanding for at least a second time…'* (Ofsted, 2009). Leaders in these schools tend to be risk takers without being rash. They have *'professional, social and emotional intelligence'* (Mongon and Chapman, 2012) which, combined with a personal sense of self-efficacy, enables them to engage in radical practice of the kind which David Hargreaves has called 'disciplined innovation' (Hargreaves, 2003).

Although schools serving communities with similar levels of deprivation can deliver very different outcomes, the attainment gap between pupils from different social backgrounds in England remains obstinately resistant to significant reduction:

> If you want to know how well a child will do at school, ask how much its parents earn. The fact remains, after more than 50 years of the welfare state and several decades of comprehensive education, that family wealth is the single biggest predictor of success in the school system.
>
> (Hatcher, 2006)

Independent research shows that the attainment gap between rich and poor in England not only persists but actually widens the longer children are in school (Feinstein, 2003; Goodman and Gregg, 2010). Government statistics only confirm that phenomenon:

> The best odds of a FSM [free school meal] pupil achieving the expected standard occur in the Foundation Stage, and even then the odds are that they are two and a half times less likely to achieve it than the more affluent pupils. The odds for FSM pupils worsen at the end of Key Stage (KS) 1 and remain stable at about three times less likely to achieve the expected standard in Key Stage 2 and through to age 19.
>
> (DCSF, 2009a: 15)

The Department for Children, Schools and Families' (DCSF) use of proportions in the quote above obscures the increasing size of the gap between children entitled to free school meals and others which is illustrated in Figure 1.1. The 16 per cent gap between those aged 7 reaching national 'target' levels at the end of Key Stage 1 has increased to 28 per cent by the age of 16 at the end of Key Stage 4.

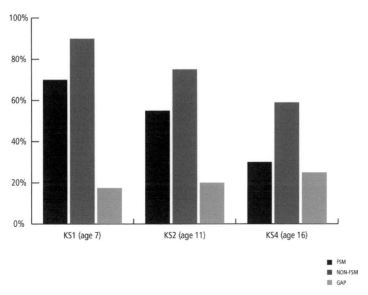

Figure 1.1: Percentages achieving 'national target levels' at the end of each Key Stage by FSM entitlement

Source: Department for Education (DfE, 2010b)

Even as the performance of the whole 16-year-old cohort has improved over recent years, the gap between FSM and non-FSM students has stuck at just below 30 per cent (Figure 1.2).

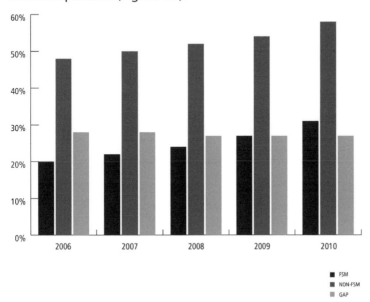

Figure 1.2: Percentage achieving GCSE 5 A*–C including English and maths in Year 11 by FSM entitlement

Source: DfE (2010b)

Free School Meal (FSM) eligibility is the proxy for socio-economic status used in national data and in some research. It has its critics as a proxy and may underestimate the effect of comparative wealth and poverty. Using the same standard – the pass rate of 5 A*–C at GCSE including English and maths – the gap has been reported as approaching 50 percentage points (74.1 per cent vs 26.8 per cent) between the children from 'higher managerial and professional' families and those from families where the adults are employed in routine or semi-routine labour (Strand, 2009). The gap is higher where there is long-term unemployment. According to central government's analyses the extent of the series of gaps across social classes – defined by parental occupation – should be a cause for even greater concern (Figure 1.3). The average attainment levels reported for each of the five occupational groups in Figure 1.3 are higher than any of the attainment levels for the FSM group reported in Figure 1.2. This suggests that poverty, of which FSM entitlement is arguably a measure, may have an independently significant influence on student outcomes.

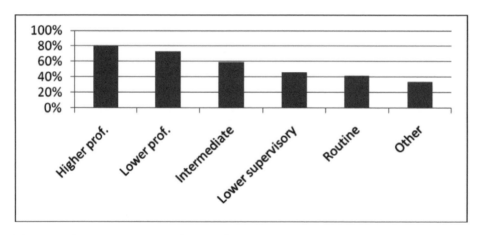

Figure 1.3: Percentages achieving GCSE 5 A*–C by parental occupation

Source: DCSF (2008a: Table 4.1.2)

At the end of their school careers, students from 'upper socio-economic backgrounds' are twice as likely to enter university as students from 'lower socio-economic background' (PAC 2009: 9). There is also some evidence that socio-economic gaps in educational outcomes have been greater in the UK than in many economically advanced countries (OECD, 2001).

Although the gap between rich and poor students is the widest and most persistent gap in the English system that does not mean it is the only one which should cause concern. The persistently low average performance of students from Black Caribbean backgrounds and the even poorer average performance of White British students from families where employment is 'routine, semi routine or non-existent' also demand attention (Strand, 2008 and 2009). Figure 1.4 shows outcomes for students in another minority group, those at each of the four levels defining special educational need (SEN) in schools in England. In broad terms those levels are: pupils with no identified need; pupils with needs that should be met by the school (School Action); pupils whose needs should be met by the school with some support (School Action Plus); and pupils whose needs have to be formally recognised and met by local authority intervention in special or mainstream settings (pupils with SEN statements). It would be remarkable, odd even, if the average attainment of pupils with special educational need was not below average national levels for those with no identified need. However, it is arguable whether anyone could be content with gaps as wide and as persistent as those revealed in Figure 1.4.

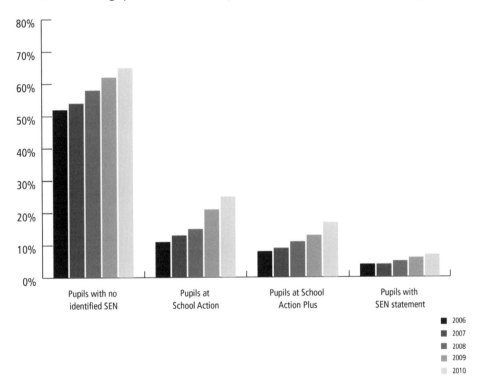

Figure 1.4: Percentage of students achieving GCSE 5 A*–C including English and maths at the end of KS4, 2006–10 by SEN level

Source: DfE (2010b)

Finally, the attainment of looked after children (LAC) is perhaps the most disappointing underperformance for the public education service. The gap between LACs and other students at GCSE 5 A*–C including English and maths has been persistently close to 40 percentage points right through the first decade of this century. In 2000, *'only 7.3% of looked-after children attained 5 GCSE passes at grades A*–C'* (DoH, 2001). Ten years later 12 per cent of LACs achieved five or more GCSEs or the equivalent, including English and maths at grades A* to C (DfE, 2010c). Behind those 'end of schooling' comparisons the data from early years and primary school assessments reveals the stark fact that the longer looked after children, those for whom we have a common responsibility, are in contact with schools and other services, the poorer their performance is likely to be in comparison with their peers.

The moral challenge and pragmatic waste of resources inherent in these persistent inequalities are reasons why the innovations developed by the schools profiled in this book matter so much: they have dared to try social innovations – new and more effective ways to promote learning – in order to tackle often deep-seated inequalities. They have innovated by pitching themselves into the heart of some of the most contentious questions about the respective roles of schools, families and communities in determining how improvements in educational outcomes come about.

The international perspective

These disparities are not solely an English or even a British phenomenon – they are international. Large disparities in educational attainment exist in many countries *'and are heavily influenced by the type of school students attend and their family backgrounds'* (UNESCO, 2010: 19). Although numbers are falling (sadly at a reducing rate), an estimated 72 million primary age children do not attend school at all and the number is similar for young people of secondary age (ibid.:12 and 14). Wide gender disparity persists with marked variations between and even within regions (p13). In 26 countries, UNESCO reports, 20 per cent or more of those aged 17 to 22 have had fewer than two years of schooling, and in some countries, the share is 50 per cent or more. Marginalisation may be a consequence of attitudes to gender (for girls more than boys), economy (for rural groups more than urban), language (for example Kurdish speaking groups in Turkey) or other factors. It is not a phenomenon confined to poorer countries: in the European Union as a whole, 15 per cent of young people have only lower secondary school education (30 per cent in Spain). In the USA, African-Americans are twice as likely to be out of school as white Americans, and young adults from poor households are three times as likely to be out of school as those from wealthy homes. *'Although the USA ranks ninth out of forty-eight countries on the TIMSS scale for mathematics… the lowest 10% of performers in the United States fall below the average for Thailand and Tunisia'* (UNESCO, 2010: 24).

UNESCO's report concluded:

> *School-based disparities do not operate in isolation. In many cases they interact with and reinforce wider disadvantage. Parental income and education, home language and other factors are all*

strongly associated with learning achievement... In countries with more equitable systems, children's backgrounds are less important in determining achievement. Where there is a strong relationship between student background and performance, or where large differences in student backgrounds exist, reducing differences in school quality is unlikely to be enough to improve equity significantly.

(UNESCO, 2010: 19)

However, just like schools – though on a larger scale – countries vary in their outcomes and in their capacity to buck the trends. When schools buck the trend, we all ask, how do they do that and why can't everyone do it? The same questions can be raised at an international level though we might then expect the same complex and uncertain responses! From that broader, international perspective, one of the most inspiring examples of success comes from Finland, which regularly figures in the top three in most subjects covered by the authoritative PISA rankings of educational performance (Hautamäki *et al.*, 2008: passim).

In a world-class system like Finland's, socioeconomic standing is far less predictive of student achievement. All things being equal, a low-income student in the United States is far less likely to do well in school than a low-income student in Finland. Given the enormous economic impact of educational achievement, this is one of the best indicators of equal opportunity in a society.

(McKinsey, 2009: 9)

About 96 per cent of Finnish school students complete their education; only 2 per cent repeat a year and only 0.5 per cent drop out (Lankinen, 2009). Yet Finland only spends the average of OECD countries on education – about 6 per cent of Gross Domestic Product (GDP). Finnish children spend less time in school than their peers in other countries: school does not start till the age of seven and even then children spend at most 190 days per year at school, for between four and seven hours per day, less than in many other OECD countries. The Finnish system is both highly equitable – there is no purposeful streaming or selection – and very high quality (Lankinen, 2009). One key factor in this sustained high performance appears to be that Finland attracts good people into teaching, which is a highly regarded profession: only 10 per cent of applicants for teacher training are accepted. At school, teachers are able to devote additional time to students who need extra help and there is enough flexibility in a broad curriculum to provide for different styles of learning. Teachers have a strong professional commitment to collaborative, interactive forms of learning, promoting problem solving and critical thinking, as well as to basic skills such as reading, which has a high priority (Aho *et al.*, 2006; Välijärvi *et al.*, 2007). Other successful schools and education systems have these ingredients: good people attracted into teaching, career-long learning that is well supported, creativity that is encouraged and problem solving which is the basis of professionals' work with children (Whelan, 2009).

Yet for many countries this Finnish recipe remains just an aspiration: recreating the recipe and getting the right balance of ingredients is difficult. Following Finland would mean doing more than investing in better teachers. Finland is a small, highly socially and culturally homogeneous and relatively consensual society; its culture cannot be replicated easily. The Finnish approach would take many years to work (Barber and Mourshed, 2007) and cash injection is not a plausible alternative. In the US spending per child in education rose by 70 per cent in 25 years but produced no appreciable improvement in literacy rates (Hanushek, 1998). School spending there is among the least cost effective in the world and costs 60 per cent more than the average for other wealthy nations for each point scored on the PISA maths test (McKinsey, 2009: 9). In the UK, despite doubling state spending for education and training in the past 20 years, around 30,000 children a year continue to leave school with few if any qualifications. In France the failures of mass schooling are most evident in the high rates of grade repetitions and drop outs among children from poorer, ethnic minority suburbs (Whelan, op. cit.).

The compelling case for innovation

On first reading, the challenges of the developed and developing worlds are quite different. The challenge in the developing world is to provide low cost but effective learning, on a vast scale, to hundreds of millions of poor families in societies where education is not yet systemic. The challenge in the developed world is to tackle deep-rooted underperformance and inequality, as well as to make learning fit for the times. But what these challenges have in common is that they are created by ingrained and universally expensive historic failings. They have not been amenable to what Heifetz (Heifetz and Linsky, 2002) and later Fullan (Fullan, 2005) might characterise as *technical solutions* – the application of school effectiveness techniques from the current research or policy lexicon. They require *adaptive approaches* (ibid.) which operate outside current understanding or practice. In Europe and the United States, nineteenth-century urbanisation depended on and municipalised social innovations that would make cities bearable: not least public libraries, parks, public transport, communal waste disposal and mass schooling. Societies in the developing world will need radical social innovation on a similar scale. Societies in the developed world will need to deliver on the promise to offer social mobility and economic improvement which has failed for significant numbers of children.

In the context of teaching, across the globe the medium is also the message: governments face the challenge of whether school systems inherited from the industrial era can provide the capabilities – for curiosity, collaboration and creativity – that are needed in modern, innovation-driven economies. There is a danger that if schools teach children to pass tests and exams they will not impart the social and entrepreneurial skills that the children will need to prosper. Schools might be hitting the target but missing the point. This means that accelerating change through central initiatives, as we will argue in Chapter 3, generates its own downsides and eventually bumps up against a glass ceiling of its own making, frustrated by the eventual incoherence and lack of local or personal commitment to which centralism is prone. That is why policy makers and practitioners are increasingly looking elsewhere for solutions. Innovation to improve education services is essential, but it is a long struggle. The most obvious places to look are not just in schools but where children do most of their learning, particularly their early formative learning: in communities and families.

It is a universal truth insufficiently celebrated that schools are neither the only, nor necessarily the most important places where children learn (see Bentley, 1998). Children learn first in their homes, families and communities. Children's home backgrounds crucially affect their capacity and resources for learning. Economist James Heckman's work shows that children deprived of opportunities to learn in their early years are very difficult to reach as teenagers (Heckman, 1995; Heckman *et al.*, 2006). In Harlem the poorest children arrive in school with an average of 25-hours of independent reading behind them. The average middle class child in America has 1,700 hours and their vocabulary is twice as large (Dobbie and Fryer, 2009). Middle-class children are six times more likely to be praised than the poorest children (Heckman, 1995). The development of literacy and numeracy skills in childhood is a good predictor of later educational attainment and subsequent earnings. A substantial body of research shows that children from middle-class families are far more likely to develop both cognitive skills like literacy, and social and emotional capacities, for example the ability to apply oneself to work and get on with others (Lexmond and Reeves, 2009). Children from poorer backgrounds who score highly in tests at 22 months are overtaken by lower-scoring children from affluent backgrounds by the age of six or seven (Feinstein, 2003). Half the gap between affluent and deprived children's educational performance can be explained by the home environment. Poorer parents are likely to have fewer material resources for learning, including books and writing material. Poverty also puts people under pressure, and so the emotional stress of living in a poor household can also have an impact on parenting and learning (Becker, 1981; Becker and Tomes, 1986; Blau, 2008; Elder and Caspi, 1988; Conger *et al.*, 1999). The connections between these factors and learning are complex but clear: a child's ability to learn is affected by social and emotional well-being. Parental support and encouragement are vital once they attend school to deepen and extend what they learn. Sibling role models can play a critical role in shaping attitudes towards learning. That is why many argue that the right approach is not to focus exclusively on schools but on how schools need support in the form of initiatives to promote learning in families.

But of course families are not the sole influence. The communities in which families live also matter. Rich and poor communities have very different resources for learning. Often they provide very different environments: for example, access to a library where a child feels safe to go after school. We are learning more about how social networks and peer influences shape behaviour and outlook (Christakis and Fowler, 2010). School may make only a limited impact on children if, when they leave, they go back to disinvested communities facing huge social and economic challenges. Advocates of a greater focus on community argue that schools and teachers are often asked to deal with issues that originate outside the classroom. Combating poverty and improving communities may have more long-run pay offs and thus make it easier for schools to perform. In the US a string of studies over the past 50 years or so has argued that most of the differences in performance in school tests are actually attributable to community and environmental factors (Coleman *et al.*, 1966; Fryer and Levitt, 2004). Schools are limited in the enhancement they can offer to young people's life chances unless the community they live and work in also improves.

Hills and Stewart (2005) summarise the complex interaction of factors by suggesting the following connections to explain how unemployment, poverty and ill-health contribute to segregation and low educational achievement.

A low level of family income can directly affect children by:

- determining the quality of child care
- limiting resources for additional tuition
- limiting school choice by preventing moves to preferred catchment areas
- impairing a child's health
- deterring continuing post-compulsory education.

A low level of parental education can affect:

- the parents' interest in education
- parents' ability to help with school work
- children's motivation and aspiration
- a child's development.

'Deprived areas' can affect children's attainment by:

- influencing aspiration and motivation through the level and quality of local employment
- creating problems in recruiting and retaining teachers
- simply hampering learning opportunities
- nurturing a culture of low achievement and negative peer pressure
- limiting extra-curricular activity.

Each of these contributory elements – school, family and community – has powerful advocates and bodies of evidence to support its claim to be the key factor. The academic disputes between these positions have sometimes been fractious, the political arguments ferocious and professional disagreements contentious. The local activities profiled in this book matter because they plunge themselves right into the heart of this heated debate by trying to find a creative combination of these traditions and insights.

Chapter 2

Work in progress

In England and internationally, the state's concern for the education of its citizens is still a work in progress. Our taken-for-granted belief that this is a legitimate area for government may be a lifetime's experience for us but it is a relatively new phenomenon in the broad sweep of human history and a mainly twentieth-century phenomenon at that. We are still learning about learning: what the education service is for and what the government's role should be is a contested area in many countries. Its social implications, its cost and its potential benefits make it the stuff of national politics across the world. Writing with Annika Wong, one of us recently proposed that there are four basic strategies which governments in the developing and developed world can pursue to meet the kinds of challenges described in Chapter 1 – improve, reinvent, supplement, and transform schools and learning (Leadbeater and Wong, 2010). That work drew on and describes an extensive range of international examples illustrating each of the four key strategies. In this chapter we will use the four as the first part of an exploration of how the work of our ten schools can be contextualised in a broader perspective. We will then introduce three key drivers which underpin innovative activity and which can be used to analyse the schools' work.

A grid and four strategies

The four identified strategies are based on the assumption that learning can take place in informal or formal settings and that innovation can be technical or disruptive. Internationally, the learning of the 70 million primary-age children and 70 million young people of secondary age who do not attend school is inevitably taking place in informal settings. Even those who do learn in formal settings spend only a small proportion of their childhood hours in their classrooms, schools or colleges. That is not only true in the developing world, it is also true in England where pupils and students spend less than a quarter of their waking hours in formal settings. Relying on good schools will not be enough in either context. Ensuring enhancement of the intrinsic quality of informal context as well as their contribution to the work of the formal settings should be a priority for any educational agency.

'Technical innovation' improves an existing organisation or product by making it more effective. As e-technology replaces the exercise books and pens which once replaced slates and chalk, as interactive whiteboards replace blackboards, it is easy to point to some technical innovation in school life. 'Disruptive innovation' is less easy to identify in the national school systems which were founded in the early twentieth century, although they were themselves often disruptive in their origins. In the UK, our familiarity with distance learning should not cause us to forget just how contested and disruptive the foundation of the Open University's innovative distance learning programmes were in 1969! Examples of disruptive innovation are more common in the less rigidly controlled developing systems (Leadbeater and Wong, op. cit.).

The juxtaposition of formal and informal with technical and disruptive can be visualised through the simple grid shown in Table 2.1 which should help us to explore the different strategies available to governments, schools and families for innovation in learning.

Table 2.1: The education innovation grid

	Formal learning	Informal learning
Technical innovation	IMPROVE	SUPPLEMENT
Disruptive innovation	REINVENT	TRANSFORM

The top left-hand cell (IMPROVE) points us to the most common approach, at least in developed economies: 'technical innovation' applied to the improvement of formal settings such as schools and colleges. The school improvement agenda absorbs academic effort and is adopted by governments around the world – enrolling more children into better schools, with better leaders, improved teaching and enhanced facilities – and fits into this category. As more children internationally attend school and as, in England, absence rates are driven down, what happens inside traditional schools, the activity of teaching and learning, will remain vitally important. Later chapters in this book will record how the schools recognise that their core compact with the families and children they serve is based on the quality of teaching and learning they provide. If that is not good enough, then the community is unlikely to be convinced that the school can be useful in other ways.

The top right-hand cell (SUPPLEMENT) brings us to 'technical innovation' applied to supplement or enhance informal learning – that is, learning outside school with peers, family and community settings. This is innovation which creates spaces for learning where they are needed, rather than just using schools, and starts the learning from people's life experience rather than from a formal curriculum. This quadrant is attracting growing attention from policy makers for all the reasons we mentioned in Chapter 1: families and communities have a huge bearing on whether children are ready or able to learn at school. Later chapters in this book will report how the PV schools see this as a two-way street – the school's capacity to enhance local learning in one direction and, from the opposite direction, the community's capacity to contribute to the school's more formal work.

The bottom left-hand cell (REINVENT) introduces 'disruptive innovation' into formal learning – the mandate to reinvent school. Reinvented schools might have teachers, assessments and classes, but they might be radically different from the traditional school in other ways. For example:

- governance, the relationship between the professional providers and the community they work for, may be designed in new ways
- timetables might be more personalised
- assessment might be formative rather than summative
- classes might be organised around ability and interest rather than age
- learning might be less didactic, more collaborative with an emphasis on problem solving
- there might be more peer-to-peer teaching and learning
- the architecture and use of buildings might create variety in the school day and in the spaces where learning happens.

Governments and educational entrepreneurs around the world are making growing investment in these areas to create schools fit for the twenty-first century. Later chapters in this book will show how schools can reinvent governance and relationships between teachers and taught, sometimes redefining the meanings of 'teacher' and 'taught'.

The bottom right-hand cell (TRANSFORM) brings 'disruptive innovation' into informal learning outside school. This is not found in alternative types of school but in alternatives to school, which make learning available without a school structure, classroom, teacher, timetable or exam. The schools in this study have not yet stepped into this quadrant and it would be difficult for schools in the English system to do so. By pointing towards supplementation and reinvention their work is an indicator of how parts of the system can at least move beyond the narrow paradigm of improvement towards transformation.

We have used the innovation grid to contextualise the work of the ten schools reported in this study. We think that their work, by illustrating alternatives to the formal, systemic approaches to which most schools in England adhere, has something to offer to both developed and developing educational systems. For the former they demonstrate that there are optional and successful paradigms which, although not without risk, can be adopted with success. Internationally, they offer encouragement that there are alternatives to the school-based industrial model of schooling and that local solutions can transcend educational policy and fads.

In summary, we believe that the work reported in later chapters is important for several reasons.

- On its own, improvement in our current schools will not be enough to meet the growing and changing demands of government, commerce, parents and children.
- We deceive ourselves if we do not grasp that this is as true of the established school systems of the developed world as it is of the much more recently created mass school systems in the developing world. It is even true of schools defined as 'successful' within the dominant designs of established systems.
- Strategies that supplement and support learning at school by working with families and in communities – to change habits, culture, values and aspirations – will become increasingly important.
- Education needs more powerful sources of disruptive innovation to create different kinds of schools and to create alternatives to school – in effect to create entirely new ways to learn.
- Disruptive innovation in education is often weak because state regulation, teacher union power, parental conservatism and political micromanagement create high barriers to new entry ideas. Creating diverse new ways for people to learn is still too difficult and over dependent on maverick individuals. Disruptive innovation needs more support and encouragement.
- Disruptive, radical innovation rarely comes from the mainstream. Most often it comes from renegades and outsiders working in the margins.
- Radical approaches appear more likely to emerge from the developing world but may be equally applicable in the developed world. The same is true of the small amount of disruptive innovation in established systems – it may be transferable to developing contexts.
- In established systems, disruptive innovation may not come from the highest-attaining schools. It is much more likely to come from social and educational entrepreneurs who seek to meet huge need without the resources for traditional solutions.
- Governments should continue to look to the very best school systems to guide improvement strategies while simultaneously looking to their own social entrepreneurs operating at the structural and cultural margins.

Discovering innovative capacity, authorising environment and measurement

In order to move out of the 'improvement' quadrant of the innovation grid, most public service innovations, including those we will describe later, involve three core ingredients (Figure 2.1). They are:

- a favourable *authorising environment* to support the risk taking involved in innovation
- the availability of *new capacity* to support new approaches to a need
- appropriate *measures of value* to demonstrate the impact of innovation on targeted outcomes and to test comparisons with historical approaches.

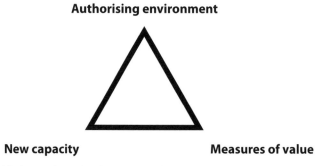

Figure 2.1: Public innovation triangle

Source: Based on Moore (1995)

Successful innovations bring these three ingredients together and strengthen them, expanding the scope for successful innovation to be scaled up. Good impact provides the basis for a more favourable environment and that in turn allows for investment in additional capacity – a virtuous spiral is created. We need to explain each of these three elements before using them as the basis for reflection on the schools' work. The components of the triangle will help us to explain what these schools are doing, their achievements and the challenges they face.

Authorising environment

To be successful, public services innovation has to be protected by an authorising environment which supports the case for innovation and the risks involved. Innovation involves taking risks and accepting uncertainty. It is impossible to say in advance whether an innovation will succeed. In public services, innovation inevitably has a political component. Unless that component is translated into an authorising mandate providing public servants with the permissions to take risks, to try something different that is not in a manual, then the innovation will be stifled by caution and insecurity. Creating an environment that encourages innovation is partly the role of politicians, national and local, including school governors. It is partly the job of policy makers to create spaces in which innovation is allowed and encouraged. Professional peers can also help set the context for innovation, lending it credibility. The schools in this report often set out actively to manage the wider political environment in which they were innovating – creating alliances, winning over partners, gaining endorsement from figures of authority. Slowly the environment for this kind of innovation is, overall, becoming more favourable.

In England, the three main political parties are all committed at least to the rhetoric of localism, devolving more and more discretion directly to councils, communities and service users to pool budgets and commission services directly. The Labour Government articulated this through its Every Child Matters policies and the introduction of Children's Trusts and Children's Services Departments. It explored similar themes by sponsoring the Total Place project (Total Place, 2010), a striking and promising example of this trend, which allowed all public spending in an area to be brought together to achieve shared outcomes. At the time of writing, the Coalition Government is in turn exploring the themes: in education through its commitment to school autonomy and more widely through its Big Society programme. Increased local autonomy will allow schools greater opportunities for collaboration with other public and private organisations (DfE, 2011a). The Big Society programme sets out to give citizens, communities and local government the power and information they need to come together and solve the problems they face, in particular by transferring power to become more local and by encouraging people to take an active role in their communities (Cabinet Office, 2010).

So the authorising environment for the innovative approaches of these schools has been improving. Once considered marginal, they have found that the mainstream is moving in their direction, seeking more joined up, community-based initiatives that promote behaviour change and build capacity in communities as well as delivering services to them. It remains to be seen whether that direction of travel can be maintained by semi-autonomous schools that are increasingly focused on the internal requirements of core teaching and learning.

New capacity

Most innovation involves the creation of new capacity: a new technology, process or way of working. Innovation might also involve the combination of existing technologies and processes in new ways. The schools in this study have not invented entirely new programmes; they have created new combinations of existing programmes, to make new educational recipes.

They are hybrid mixes of schools, social enterprises, parenting, after school and community programmes. Few if any of the individual ingredients are new, but the combination of them is. This book is largely an account of how and why these combinations have been put together and the mix of skills and leadership involved. Invariably these schools have been responding to issues on their doorstep – trying to tackle issues in the lives of families which affect the learning of children at the school. Their commitment to better outcomes has driven them to look beyond school for solutions.

Community-based services, however, will have to respond to community concerns, just as these schools in the public value enquiry have done, rather than taking their cue from national standards and programmes. That will require more flexibility, judgement and initiative on the part of people leading these initiatives. The growing interest of policy makers in promoting behaviour change among service users, as well as more efficient delivery of services, should also play to the strengths of activities like those which try to engage families and communities to invest more and more consistently in learning. Their aim is not simply to deliver a better service to children but to persuade families to change their outlook and behaviour towards learning. One of the main routes to achieve that is through peer-to-peer influences on behaviour, building on social networks in society. In other words the best way to get parents to invest more time, effort and commitment in their children's education may be through the role modelling and support of other parents rather than by providing better teachers.

Underlying all of this is a much bigger picture of how public services generate better outcomes for society. The main focus on public services has been on compliance and performance: how services comply with standards and reach targets which in turn drive improved performance and outcomes. Improving performance by moving people closer to higher standards of performance is seen as a question of improved processes and quality, driven by inspection and regulation, investment in higher skills and better facilities. Yet the outcomes that societies seek – better health, safer communities, a cleaner environment – cannot be delivered by public services on their own. They come from adaptable, capable and resilient communities, able to organise themselves in more effective ways. As well as better public services we need more adaptive and resilient communities and, crucially, we need both to work together.

Measurement

The third ingredient for successful public-services innovation is measurement, to audit the limitations of current, standard approaches and to show the value created by new approaches. Innovation is more often than not a leap of faith, propelled by a sense of frustration with the status quo and a belief that better solutions are possible. Often innovation has to get started before proper evidence to support it can be assembled. It is often difficult for innovators to compete against established and familiar incumbent approaches to a problem. That is why for innovation to be sustained and to spread, its costs and benefits need to be properly measured. Innovation is an iterative process of conjecture, trial, error and adjustment. It depends on feedback to allow adjustments to be made. The authorising environment for innovation, especially innovation at scale, cannot be maintained without good evidence.

So as well as developing new programmes, services and forms of organisation, these schools have been developing new, often *ad hoc*, measures of success. By and large their approach has been to accept established measures of success based on test scores and exam outcomes while treating them as incomplete and inadequate. They need to be complemented by other measures of engagement, commitment, well-being and non-academic achievement.

Yet this shift to a different approach to measurement is fraught with challenges which are beyond the skills and scope of the schools themselves to resolve. In summary, these include:

- **The measurement of inputs**
  In schools we measure teacher to pupil ratios, days at school, materials used in classrooms. The schools in the public value enquiry were also seeking to engage parents and communities: how do you measure parental commitment, peer influence and community culture?
- **The measurement of outputs**
  In schools we commonly measure test scores and exam results, mainly focused on cognitive skills, academic fields of knowledge and end-of-course assessments which are significantly a test of memory. Are these the right outputs for a knowledge-based economy using twenty-first century technology?
- **The measurement of outcomes**
  Many schools, including those in the public value enquiry, want to contribute to outcomes such as social and emotional well-being, behaviour over lifetime, civility and community cohesion. Increasing public value might be another desirable outcome. These less tangible and often longer-term factors are more difficult to measure and to account for.
- **The measurement of processes**
  In schools the main process for transforming inputs into outputs is teaching and learning. The quality of the teaching process determines the learning outcomes. The schools in the public value enquiry engaged in processes that are more personal and based in community development. They are less predictable and more diffuse. Setting standards for them is much more problematic.

- **Determining timescales**
  The pay offs from the programmes in which the PV schools engaged may not be apparent for some time after families have engaged in them. Schools that underperform immediately come under pressure to improve. Effective improvement programmes are designed to deliver swift results in terms of exams. Activities like those sponsored by the PV schools can often only have an impact over a much longer period.
- **Selecting units of measurement**
  The units of measurement in the school are pupils, lessons and exams. They are like units in a production line: identifiable and distinct. The projects profiled in the public value enquiry, however, were also working with relationships, networks, families and communities. To properly account for their work with families and communities we would need forms of assessment that are very different from tests and exams.

Conclusion

The debate over the sources of educational inequality and underperformance has too often seemed to pitch schools, families and communities against one another. The projects in the public value enquiry were attempting to bring them together, to find ways for schools to work with families and communities both to improve educational outcomes for their pupils and to improve the quality of life in the communities in which they operate. It is the combination of improved schools, support for families and better communities which leads to sustained improvements in educational outcomes and life chances. That is why these projects are significant. The case studies in this report show schools making progress with creating these combinations, mixing skills and programmes, handling complex and overlapping relationships and accountabilities. The leaders in this work are both headteachers and community leaders – sometimes, though not always, embodied in the same person.

In the following chapters we will use the triangle of authorising environment, new capacity and measures of value to explore and reflect on the work of the schools. We will begin, in the next chapter, by recalling how the education system in England methodically nationalised and centralised each element of the triangle over the course of the twentieth century. It is a salutary reminder of how new some of the taken-for-granted features of the current system really are. We will then report how the schools and leaders in the study stepped outside the mainstream framework to create new authorisation, to develop capacity and to promote measures of value beyond the confines of academic attainment.

Chapter 3

A 'new story' for education?

The school knew it needed to play a central role in the community so that its success would have an impact locally. This impact would influence the life chances of the children, many of whom come from homes of social disadvantage. We work with our parents, the children's centre, community police, local churches, residential homes for senior citizens and local businesses. We teach core academic skills effectively to give children the educational boost they need; but we place a keen emphasis on personal development to build aspiration and promote social harmony.

Sheila Audsley, former Headteacher, Clifton Green Primary School

In an earlier piece on leadership for public value (Leadbeater and Mongon, 2008) we wrote that the education service in England was in need of a 'new story' to tell about its connection with the lives of children, young people, families and communities. We drew an analogy with playwright Tom Stoppard's treatment of two minor characters from Shakespeare's *Hamlet*. By writing about their lives outside the play and occasionally weaving his narrative with Shakespeare's he did not simply tell a 'new story', he put the spotlight on one which had been there all the time, off stage. He also provoked a profound reflection on the Shakespearean narrative we already knew. What follows might be in the same tradition, although less cleverly written. The 'new stories' might be a different way of describing some continuing historic practices but the narrative puts the spotlight on some previously underrated features of the education service and encourages a reflection on what has been emphasised about the service in recent decades. *'The reality is that innovation is invariably a collaborative and cumulative process, often drawing on older ideas and assembling novel combinations of existing ideas'* (Leadbeater, 2012: 21).

The narrative which dominated education policy for the last decade of the twentieth century and first years of the twenty-first century in England has haemorrhaged credibility. Tightening control by central government over curriculum, assessment, accountability and structure, combined with increasing competition between schools, hit a glass ceiling – and a disappointingly low ceiling at that. The efforts being made by individuals and the contribution from public funds seemed disproportionate to the outcomes for a system which remains demonstrably weak on equity and arguably short on excellence.

The inverted commas around 'new story' reflect a question about how 'new' the story might be given the strong seam of connection with neighbourhood, community and local networks which runs through the history of schooling in England. That history stretches back through the last century and deep into the one before that. What constitutes a 'new story' at the level of national policy, might feel more familiar to some schools and communities. The policy-driven version of the education service's narrative for the past quarter century or so has focused on the internal management of schools – if every school was managed with similarly efficient techniques then outcomes across schools would become similar. If there is now to be a resurgence of autonomy and the potential for schools to connect with their communities as they choose, then that might be described as not so much an innovation and more a renovation in the English system. The autonomy of individual schools from national prescription provides the opportunity for renewal of a persistent, if not widespread, tradition to which the leaders who contributed to the enquiry at the core of this book belong. They are committed to solving local problems rather than applying national solutions and to a belief in the *radically old idea* that *community and conversation are the roots of creativity* (Leadbeater, 2008b: 54).

Disconnection from community – the twentieth-century story

The twentieth-century story of English schooling is of a community enterprise gradually overrun by nationalisation and centralisation – at first randomly and slowly but then, in the final quarter of the century, with accelerated determination.

- *Authorising environments* were increasingly defined in and centralised through national legislation.
- *Capacity* was narrowed to a centrally approved, professional hegemony dependent on national funding.
- *Measures of success* became limited to a particular set of academic attainments and a narrow inspection regime.

Sponsors of the many changes which separately or collectively corralled the system into its national configuration might well have believed that, at each stage, they would be enhancing equity and excellence. If equity and excellence were the aims then, far from achieving them, centralisation has fallen short and is now a far from compelling narrative. We will also argue that, obscured by the general trends, there were exceptions which maintained and nurtured community links and from which we now have much to learn.

Disconnecting the authorising environment

Towards the end of the nineteenth century, the Elementary Education Act (1870) and the later Education Act (1880) founded the public sector education service in England by, in effect, nationalising existing local provision. Before those Acts:

- *the authorising environment* for schools not charging fees had been mainly in the hands of local activists
- *the capacity* of that part of the system depended largely on philanthropy and volunteers
- *the measures of value* commonly included the pupils' social as well as academic or technical attributes.

The iconic British model for community schooling before 1870 had emerged early in the nineteenth century, not in England but in Scotland and sponsored by a Welshman. Robert Owen, a wealthy industrialist and philanthropist, pioneered model communities in New Lanark which included infant schools, crèches, medical care and lifelong education (Donnachie, 2000). One of the more referenced examples of English provision before 1870 was another philanthropic endeavour, the Ragged School Union founded in 1844. By 1870 that Union had sponsored over 300 free schools for the poor, maintained mostly by philanthropy and volunteer community effort. Union Schools, National (Anglican Church) Schools, British (Non-conformist Church) Schools and Industrial Schools were among the complex range of local variations which emerged in the nineteenth century to provide schooling for those who could not afford places in the fee paying institutions. These 'poor schools', maintained sometimes by individual sponsors but also by churches, trade unions, mutual societies and other community groups, generally reflected their benefactors' philanthropic, evangelical, communitarian, reformist or industrial interests alongside or intertwined with the subject teaching they offered. The late nineteenth century Education Acts therefore brought a diverse and complex range of independent, voluntary and community provision into public ownership or, at least, made it subject to state supervision through local School Boards. The 1870 Education Act did not invent free or public education in England, nor did it secularise a system which then and now includes a large proportion of faith sponsored schools. The intention of the 1870 Act was, in modern terms, to supplement, systematise and quality assure the existing community effort. Robert Lowe, Vice President of the Committee of the Council on Education in Palmerston's government from 1859 to 1864 and Chancellor of the Exchequer under Gladstone from 1868 to 1873 is apocryphally quoted as saying *'we must educate our masters'* as a justification for the 1870 Elementary Education Act, following the increased enfranchisement of the 1867 Reform Act. Whether he ever did coin that phrase is arguable but he certainly said, *'If [education] is not cheap, it shall be efficient, if it is not efficient, it shall be cheap. The present is neither one nor the other'* (Hansard, 1862). Nineteenth-century efficiency would be delivered by grant payment from central government to schools for enrolment, attendance and results while cheapness would be derived *'from the greater freedom of contract we now establish, by leaving managers to make their own bargains with their own servants'* (ibid.). *Plus ça change* some of us would say.

A later Education Act in 1902 consolidated the growing system (and the capacity of central administrators to oversee it) by abolishing the 2,568 School Boards and transferring their increasing powers to 328 local education authorities founded on local boroughs or county councils. For the next 70 years or so, the authorising environment moved at a slow pace in that same centralising direction, reducing the number of local authorities and, if not shifting their powers to central government, at least increasing their accountability to national ministers and civil servants. Legislative milestones in those developments included:

- periodic rises in the age for compulsory attendance (reaching 16 in 1973)
- defining the main structural elements of the secondary system (legislating for a tripartite system in 1944 and promoting, though not legislating for, a comprehensive system from 1966 onwards).

Curriculum and pedagogy remained outside the statutory framework despite being the subject of occasional advice from central government.

The 1970s brought a fundamental acceleration to that apparently leisurely approach. Successive national governments became determined to seize the controlling mechanisms of the system and, they claimed, to liberate it from the alleged inertia of local government and professional interests.

By the 1970s, the authorising environment for schools in England, often described as being the product of a *'national system locally administered'* (Ainley, 2001: 458), had become peculiarly enigmatic. The enigma was whether or how the whole operated as a system given the obfuscation around roles and responsibilities for the different players and institutions. There was no clear or agreed definition of what the phrase *'national system locally administered'* really meant. There were substantive questions about each of the four words in that phrase: what was *nationally* determined, what was *systemically* coherent, what was *locally* designed and did *administered* mean any or all of led, directed and managed? In 1951, halfway through the twentieth century, the Ministry of Education had summarised the approach as a *'progressive partnership'* aiming to provide a single, diverse and certainly not uniform system, raising standards while knitting schools more closely into the life of a democratic, industrialised community. Above all, the Ministry reported that it *'valued the life of institutions more highly than systems and has been jealous for the freedom of schools and teachers'* (Ministry of Education, 1951: 1).

This approach left unasked, or anyway unanswered, at least two key questions: what therefore are the local authorities and the school governing bodies for and what are the powers of the headteacher? The limits of a headteacher's authority were remarkably imprecise although in general terms they were the lead professional in each school with the formal authority to control its internal organisation and to supervise teaching staff (Ministry of Education, 1944). That did not mean all headteachers were actively involved in the detail of what happened in their schools. There was, in effect, a collusive authorisation between central government, local councils and professional organisations. Teachers' personal approaches were often the main source of classroom craft, curriculum and assessment (except where exams for secondary selection at 11+ demanded a focused approach). Pay and conditions of service were subject to national agreements. The local authorities usually decided on the admissions criteria, staff numbers and budget allocations but rarely became involved in the professional aspects of their schools' activities. There was *'a great fog about what school governors are entitled to do'* (Corbett, 1972: 282). Many governing bodies were confined (and some confined themselves) to a mainly social and morale boosting role around the calendar rituals of Prize Day, Summer Fete and Christmas Bazaar. This collusion began to unravel as parental dissatisfaction, commercial impatience and academic research combined to expose an education service with too many easily satisfied and underperforming providers.

> It became clear that the 'jealous protection of freedom for schools and teachers' had either created a space in which great, innovative practice could flourish or it had created a vacuum which nature abhorred, depending very much on where your children went to school or which school employed you.
>
> (Mongon and Chapman, 2012)

The question about roles and responsibilities could no longer be ignored when finally, in the mid-1970s, a furore around William Tyndale primary school in Islington coincided with the frustration of a Labour Prime Minister and former Chancellor, Jim Callaghan. The teaching staff at the primary school were alleged to have adopted a 'progressive approach' and 'free methods' at the expense of pupils'learning and to the annoyance of governors and parents (Jackson and Gretton, 1976; Conway, 2010: Ch1). At the heart of the arguments was a series of multi-linear disputes between the Department for Education, the Inner London Education Authority (ILEA), the national inspectorate, school governors, parents and staff about who was accountable for the work of the school. It was not clear who, if anyone, had the duty or powers to intervene or whether an intervention could be made in both or either of the governance and professional leadership of the school. Following the suspension of the head and some members of staff, a highly critical Committee of Enquiry confirmed that there was endemic confusion about responsibility and authority across the system (Auld, 1976). The head and some other members of staff were eventually dismissed by ILEA which was, itself, severely criticised for its initial inertia by the very enquiry it had established.

In the meantime, Jim Callaghan had taken his concerns about the education system with him from the Treasury to 10 Downing Street where he discovered that, even in the country's most senior political role, to all intents and purposes he still had no leverage to change a school system which he believed was failing and, not least, failing poorer children. In a speech at Ruskin College Oxford in 1976 Callaghan signalled his impatience and a change from the historic culture of 'partnership' towards 'accountability'. An enquiry into school governance subsequently commissioned by central government (HMSO, 1977) reported that *'the extent to which managing and governing bodies carried out the functions assigned to them in rules and articles was slight. In many areas they did not, in any real sense, exist at all'* (para 2.11). The report recommended that the options were to reform, replace or abolish governing bodies (para 3.3) and that *'...there is no area of the school's activities in respect of which the governing body should have no responsibility nor one on which the head and staff should be accountable only to themselves or to the local education authority'* (para 3.15).

Since then, the authorising environment for the education service has been increasingly characterised by central government holding local councils, school governors and headteachers accountable for the curriculum, standards and return on the investment made from public funds into the education service. Central government in England, both Labour and Conservative, has employed the rhetoric of increasing school autonomy alongside elements of competition akin to marketisation (while in reality there was increasing central control of the curriculum, assessment and accountability (Phillips and Walford, 2006)). 'Freedoms' are therefore commonly defined in terms of a statutory mandate requiring something to be done or to be not done. The contradictions embedded in this approach to authorising environments were evident in the 1988 Education Reform Act. This was the legislative apotheosis of policy development over the previous decade. It introduced 'Local Management of Schools' by enforcing the delegation to schools of budgets previously held by LEAs and created the 'National Curriculum' by providing the Secretary of State with powers to determine what schools should teach.

> *On the one hand, the government had taken central control of the curriculum and national testing but had de-centralised spending and management. In fact, the devolution of funding was designed not so much to empower schools, but to reduce the power of local authorities… So while the 1988 Act appears to devolve power from government to schools, it actually increased the power of central government.*
>
> (Ward and Eden, 2009: 21)

By the first decade of the twenty-first century English state schools had become, in broad terms, quasi-autonomous organisations commissioned by central government to provide schooling to a national prescription. It seems reasonable to claim that the authorising environment for schools in 2012 would have been widely unimaginable when most of the current school leaders began their careers (NCSL, 2009). Curriculum, assessment and accountability are in the control of central government; the political, administrative and managerial authority of the 150 or so local authorities has been eroded close to the point of extinction; 25,000 or so schools have been given extensive powers over their funding and other managerial functions. After a short period in which many headteachers felt authorised only to shift their role to becoming the resources manager – the person who ensured that budgets balanced, teachers were in front of children and the roof was repaired – most schools now realise the potential of the authority delegated to them and their emphasis has shifted markedly towards professional leadership: *'…leadership and the building of professional capacity to achieve an alignment of curriculum, pedagogy and resources with the mix of learning requirements at the school level'* (Caldwell, 2008: 235–249).

Governing bodies have now been given authority over the general aims and objectives of the school, responsibility for its budgets and accountability for its targets, though much if not all of that is often enacted under the stewardship of the headteacher. Geoff Whitty's summary is that: *'even when lay governors have opinions they wish to express, it seems that they face great difficulty in making their "voice" heard, let alone in having their views taken seriously'* (Whitty *et al.*, 1998: 100). Perhaps most importantly, lay governors are unambiguously responsible for the appointment and performance management of the headteacher.

As a consequence of these changes, five key authorising environments for school leaders might be thought of in broadly the following way (based on Mongon and Chapman, 2012: Ch 5):

- *Personal authorisation* is based to a large degree in the leaders' own attitudes and values. These are the permissions which each leader gives to others and the demands they make on themselves.
- *Associate authorisation* draws deeply on the personal connections which leaders nurture between themselves, the adults and the children who are working together daily. Leadership is a more profound quality when the group attributes it to or confers it on a person than when it is imposed on the group.
- *Institutional authorisation* is provided to *high-leverage leaders* by the governance arrangements to which they owe their primary legal accountability. These are mainly school governing bodies, though other arrangements are emerging in the English system.
- *Contextual authorisation* is created when school leaders expand their sphere of influence into the neighbourhood and professional communities around their school. In the absence of legally determined formulae for the governance of collaborative activity, *high-leverage leaders* create *ad hoc*, fit-for-purpose arrangements.
- *National authorisation* is produced by the occasionally contrary combination of legal framework, statutory targets and policy rhetoric which central government wraps around school leaders.

Three of these authorisations, personal, associate and contextual, depend to a large degree on the disposition of individual leaders. Institutional and national authorisations are less flexible though still not beyond the influence of individual leaders who constantly work to adapt and domesticate them.

A key question for the system is how should the relationship, the balance of power and the strength of accountability between these authorising environments develop? Before reporting how the school leaders and communities in the enquiry group tackled that question, we need to reflect briefly on how the development of capacity and measures of value were also disconnected from local contexts over the last century.

Disconnecting new capacity

This section will be confined to reflecting on the nationalisation and centralisation of capacity in three areas – funding, pedagogy and leadership. The characteristically different change in the role of parents – from partners in a communal enterprise to consumers of a marketed commodity – deserves a fuller consideration at another time. We do however acknowledge that change as one of the contextual factors which the school leaders whose work we are to describe had to confront. The narratives of the points we do emphasise – funding, teaching and leadership – follow a similar trajectory to authorisation: a largely weak national influence until, in the last quarter of the century, centralised control became the dominant theme.

Funding

In 2009–10, central government grants relating to education in England funded over 91 per cent of the LEAs' £41.3 billion revenue expenditure on education. Central government additionally funded 93 per cent of the local government spending of £6.1 billion on capital projects for education (Treasury, 2011: Ch 7). With those levels and proportions of national investment, the Treasury and central government cannot be neutral or diffident about what is expected in return.

We are still some distance away from reviving the national system of payment by results which characterised the later decades of the nineteenth-century education service in England, even if some commentators think we are en route towards it. In Victorian England per capita student payments were minimised and payments for teaching salaries eliminated, to be replaced by payments for students passing examinations, administered by inspectors, in reading, writing and arithmetic. This system was already being replaced by the turn of the century though aspects of it persisted for some years. The twentieth-century funding story perhaps begins with the 1918 Education Act which introduced a unified system for supporting LEA schemes by simplifying the 50 or more grants then in existence and, in effect, squeezing local philanthropy to the margins. An unfortunate postscript to that change was the austerity which prevented most LEAs from implementing statutorily required schemes for ensuring 'progressive development and comprehensive organisation of education' in their area. Education finance was further simplified in the 1944 Education Act which retained the principle of a percentage grant supplemented by special grants for particular purposes. From 1958 the main hypothecated grant was subsumed in a general grant for all local services so that LEAs would have greater autonomy in operating their range of services – of which education was only one. The requirement of the 1988 Education Act for the delegation to schools of 'their' budget share then exposed the considerable local variations in school funding, some of which still persist and currently fuel the policy interest in a single national pupil funding formula (DfE, 2010d: Ch 8). Before 1988, the government had tried to use funding to drive curriculum change through its Technical and Vocational Education Initiative (TVEI). Funding was channelled, not from the Department of Education but from the Department of Employment, through a central agency, The Manpower Services Commission. The funding was targeted on encouraging schools to improve and increase the provision of technical and vocational education. Local authorities were, for the first time and at least initially, bypassed and funding was available directly to responsive schools. The scheme was controversial in both implementation and evaluation but seminal for the government's subsequent policies for school funding.

The mandatory introduction of budget delegation to schools in 1988 was a dramatic example of central government's new found determination to use its budget powers to drive its policy changes. In a stroke it successfully marginalised LEAs and introduced a market element into the system. The schools' new found financial clout came with formula funding based on pupil numbers and, therefore, the threat that schools which did not attract parents, and consequently student admissions, would go to the wall. The following years saw national and local government embraced in a *pas de deux* during which many local authorities dissembled in order to maintain their budget control while central government struggled to enforce delegation. The final twist in that dance may be in current proposals for the introduction of another national formula with a remarkable re-emergence of direct payments from central government to schools.

Central government has also used its marginal capacity to create education grants for specific purposes to increase its grip on what happens in schools. This became clear with the creation of the initially benign LEA Training Grants Scheme (LEATGS) in the mid-1980s. This scheme, to promote the Department's priority for In-Service Training, shifted funding away from direct grants to Higher Education providers and towards consumers (LEAs and schools). At first, and providing that the funding was spent on training, there were few limitations on the grant which led to a marked increase in shorter, local courses and events. Over time, the priorities for funding in the grant became less and less flexible and more directed towards policy ends. Iconic amongst these has been the previous Labour Government's funding of National Strategies to raise attainment and to drive school improvement. The current Coalition Government's commitment to provide a grant for children on free school meals, initially £430 per capita in 2011 and predicted to increase over the next four years, is allied to two new accountability measures (DfE, 2011b):

- including new measures in performance tables that will capture the achievement of those pupils covered by the pupil premium
- requiring schools to publish online how they have used the premium so that parents and others are made fully aware of the progress and attainment of pupils covered by it and schools will concentrate on using it appropriately.

The general trend throughout has been for both core and marginal funding to be an increasingly influential factor in local spending decisions at LEA and school levels. To most school leaders it appeared as if there was persistently less scope for local discretion.

Pedagogy

The 1902 Education Act continued to diminish the system of inspection and payment by results which had generally sustained an approach to elementary teaching based on didactic and rote learning, tested by the recollection of facts. Teaching at that time, far from being the national graduate profession it might now claim to be, was a more local trade. *'It would be much easier for teachers [at the end of the twentieth century] to see the profession as, in some elemental sense, a unitary one than it was for their forebears, a century earlier'* (Gardner, 2002: 121).

Male and female teachers, urban and rural, public and private, elementary and secondary, unionised and non-unionised, progressive and traditional would almost certainly have very different experiences. For every one hundred pupils, there would be only one teacher who could be properly described as trained. That system is often described as dependent on the pupil–teacher role, a form of local apprenticeship, albeit certificated by the national inspectors during their school visits. The description underestimates the emerging strength of 'pupil teacher centres' encouraging collective initial training under the auspices of local School Boards or even teacher-led enterprise (Robinson, 2003: 25–32). Teaching and pedagogy was a fundamentally local construct.

As the century rolled on, central government would prescribe, directly or indirectly but increasingly, what a good teacher was and how they would teach. Although by the end of the century, there was still a range of ways to enter teaching, two dominated the field:

- a three or four year period of initial teacher training leading to a BEd or BA or
- a subject-based first degree followed by a one-year Postgraduate Certificate in Education (PGCE).

School Centre Initial Teacher Training Schemes (SCITTS) and Graduate Training Programmes (GTPs) were less well used routes in which schools were increasingly the leading partners. The significant feature of all of these programmes has been central government's increasing control over processes and outcomes.

The 'Great Debate' about schools which began in the mid-1970s did not initially identify teacher training and practice as a major problem but it soon became implicated. By 1977, the DES was publicly arguing that:

The curriculum paid too little attention to the basic skills of reading, writing, and arithmetic, and was overloaded with fringe subjects. Teachers lacked adequate professional skills, and did not know how to discipline children or to instil in them concern for hard work or good manners.

(DES, 1977: para 1.2)

There were *'widespread misgivings'* about initial training whose entrants often had *'inadequate experience and understanding of the world outside education'* and the teacher education curriculum needed to place greater emphasis *'on acquainting intending teachers with the national importance of industry and commerce and the challenges which our society as a whole must face'* (ibid., Ch 6). The 1977 Green Paper anticipated the nationalisation of initial, induction and in-service training.

By 1984 the DES had moved to challenge the hegemony of the Initial Teacher Training (ITT) institutions and to establish a Council for the Accreditation of Teacher Education (CATE) (DES, 1984). Until then, these institutions had led on entrance criteria, student numbers and course content. Inspections of teacher training courses were few, irregular, usually advisory and not published. Circular 3/84 began the national prescription of course structure, course approval at central and local level, partnerships with school and the *'relevant experience'* of teacher trainers (DES 1984). By the end of that decade, one part of the Department for Education was proclaiming that *'...how lessons are described and organised cannot be prescribed* [and] *organisation of the curriculum to deliver national curriculum requirements ... is a matter for the headteacher'* (DES, 1989: para 4.3). At the same time another part of the Department was increasing the homogeneity of the school workforce by tightening the specifications for courses and the arrangements for compliance, including arrangements for course inspections to be reported to CATE to which course providers would then be called to account.

Once started, the centralising trend continued at a pace through the next decade. In December 1991, Kenneth Clarke, then Secretary of State, commissioned 'three wise men' to review primary practice over the Christmas period. At the North of England conference in January 1992, he trailed proposals for a competence-based model of teacher preparation with new arrangements for 'partner schools'. The 'three wise men' delivered their gifts in January 1992 (Alexander *et al.*, 1992) and were followed quickly by circulars setting out the competencies expected of ITT, including curriculum and subject knowledge, class management, assessment, recording pupils' progress and continuing professional development (applied differently in primary and secondary sectors). This led, under Clarke's successors, to the establishment of the Teacher Training Agency (TTA) which, when its remit extended, became the Training and Development Agency (TDA). Funding for initial teacher training was moved from the Higher Education Funding Council and handed to the TTA. In turn, the TTA acted as the purchaser of training places using funding formulae linked to quality assessments.

Circular 4/98, setting out the standards for qualified teacher status (DfEE, 1998) claimed that the assessment of trainees would not require a mechanistic tick list approach or entail each standard being supported by its own evidence base, but that is arguably just what happened. The training of teachers had become the business of governments which were suspicious of theory or reflection and focused on pragmatic classroom craft. Standards became the means of imposing the central Department's will and establishing it as the purchaser of prescribed services: *'the process became teacher training, students were to be known as "trainees", universities as "providers", successful teaching as "compliance with standards", assessment as "auditing knowledge"'* (Ward and Eden, 2009: 113).

No account of the nationalisation of teaching would be complete without mention of the National Curriculum and the Office for Standards in Education (Ofsted). After more than a hundred years of curriculum advice without directives or control, central government, as we have noted above, began to intervene directly in curriculum with the TVEI initiative in the early 1980s. Even that direct funding became locally 'colonised' and 'domesticated', *'by progressive educators who succeeded in imposing as their main objective methods of active learning and pupils' personal development rather than securing the "rebirth of technical education", as promised at the outset by the minister concerned'* (Richardson and Wiborg, 2010). The National Curriculum introduced by the Education Reform Act of 1988 required all state schools in England to teach a defined curriculum including Religious Education and a group of core and foundation subjects. Its purpose was to standardise the content of pedagogy so that assessment could, in turn, also be standardised.

Ofsted, founded in 1992 as an adaptation of Her Majesty's Inspectorate (HMI), was to a large degree the product of central government's concern about the variability of local authority advisory and inspection services and their alleged collusion with local headteachers. Funding for those services was withdrawn from local budgets and used to establish the new national inspectorate. Ofsted's framework for inspection became increasingly prescriptive and by 2005 had become a comprehensive description of almost every aspect of a school's activity. This included detailed descriptions across a range of aspects of what constituted an outstanding, good, satisfactory or inadequate lesson. It would be a confident or foolish teacher who operated outside that frame.

The specifications for initial training, in-service training, curriculum content and classroom inspection combined to justify a claim that by the first decade of the twenty-first century, there was a system for teacher development from entry to exit and that it was increasingly homogenised and definitely nationalised.

Leadership

With governance, curriculum and teaching increasingly under control, central government in England turned its attention to school leadership. In broad terms, it needed to find the optimum compromise between the idealised model of the personal, morally driven and patriarchal (less often matriarchal) headteacher (Grace, 1995: 11) and the increasing central need to control what was happening in schools. For the 20,000 or so state schools, control won out over ideals. The National College for School Leadership (NCSL) and the National Professional Qualification for Headship (NPQH) were the most obvious consequences. The College was launched in 2000 and from 2004 until 2012 it was mandatory for prospective headteachers to hold the NPQH before their first appointment or be working towards it. It is now compulsory for first time headteachers. The College's Leadership Framework (NCSL, 2001) has gone through several iterations but its work remains *a single national focus for school leadership development and research together with professional development and support for school leaders throughout their careers'* (Ball, 2008: 139). Ball goes on to describe the processes inside this framework as entirely consonant with the style adopted by central government. This is characterised by self-managing surveillance and regulation in which the leader, at risk of becoming increasingly distant from his or her peers, becomes the manager of externally defined performance. This, in turn, risks generating an orthodoxy of the 'right kind' of leadership, a conveyor belt of clones.

This orthodoxy, combined with Ofsted inspections and league tables of results has been likened (Mongon and Chapman, 2012) to Foucault's invocation of Bentham's Panopticon, a prison designed to ensure that surveillance appears permanent, even if it is not continuous.

> *Bentham laid down the principle that power should be visible and unverifiable. Visible: the inmate will constantly have before his eyes the tall outline of the central tower from which he is spied upon. Unverifiable: the inmate must never know whether he is being looked at in any one moment but must be sure he may always be so.*
>
> (Foucault, 1977: 201)

Many school leaders often seem to be in an analogous position, constantly vigilant to be 'on message'.

Disconnecting the measures of value

We have already noted how the processes of accountability were moved away from teachers, school leaders and even to some extent from school governors. Ofsted inspections, central control of teacher development and marketisation through parental choice and league tables of school performance have been powerful factors in changing, arguably perhaps introducing, accountability for teaching and learning. Within that framework, the central questions were: for what should schools be accountable and how should that be measured? The answer was to be academic attainment and at the start of the 1990s there was some hope that formative, teacher assessment – conducted locally – would be an important feature in those measurements (TGAT, 1988).

That was not to be and by the middle of the 1990s the government had settled on the easy-to-measure, nationally validated, simple-to-report end of Key Stage results which had the 'advantage' of ready compilation into league tables. Every primary school has to concentrate on the percentage of pupils reaching Level 4 in English and maths at the age of 11. Every secondary school has the same interest in the percentage reaching GCSE 5A*–C including English and maths at the age of 16. Floor targets were occasionally raised over the next two decades and the 2010 floor target for all secondary schools, 35 per cent, is now a fraction above the published national average in 1990 for GCSE 5A*–C which did not then include the English and maths requirement. Over the same period, Ofsted inspection judgements became more dependent on published attainment scores despite factoring in an element for achievement. Schools which consistently fail to meet floor targets are the subject of focused intervention, commonly experience a forced change of leadership and are under increasing national pressure to take Academy status.

We will return to this point in Chapter 6 when we consider the enormous pressure on schools to meet the nationally approved measures of value above all.

Maintaining the community link: a parallel twentieth-century story

Our preceding description of the general trend for *authorising environments*, *new capacity* and *measures of value* to move away from local and community influence and, even more so, away from community control has skimmed the surface of a complex narrative. Not everything about the emergence of national standards and minimum expectations is negative or unwelcome. Not everything and not everywhere has succumbed to the pull of the policy-fuelled black hole at the centre of the education galaxy. A thread of localism has persisted and in some cases thrived. The school leaders with whom we worked are located in that powerful but minority tradition.

One of the iconic examples of schools at the heart of communities owes its origins to Henry Morris, Chief Education Officer in Cambridgeshire from 1922 to the early 1950s. Morris promoted community themes and lifelong learning, under the imaginative banner of 'raising the school leaving age to ninety' in the Cambridge Village Colleges which he designed to bring together the *'vital activities of village life'* and:

> [to] create out of discrete elements an organic whole; the vitality of the constituent elements would be preserved, and not destroyed, but

*the unity they would form would be a new thing. For, as in the case
of all organic unities, the whole is greater than the mere sum of the
parts. It would be a true social synthesis – it would take existing and
live elements and bring them into a new and unique relationship.*

(Morris, 1925).

This work was continued into the second half of the twentieth century, notably by local authorities in the East Midlands of England and particularly in Leicestershire's community colleges. In the 1960s and 70s, the Plowden Report's emphasis on parent participation, pre-school involvement, education priority areas and positive discrimination (Plowden, 1967) was allied with Eric Midwinter's descriptions of community education in Liverpool (Midwinter, 1972 and 1973). These contributors kindled an intellectual spark and then provided solid fuel for the community school movement in inner cities.

There was even a period of ambiguous sponsorship for partnerships and community activity in the policies of the past Labour Government: ambiguous, because it offered no respite from the focus on nationally measured attainment and appeared to be a diversion for many school leaders. Amongst these were broad-based neighbourhood projects – *'"area-based initiatives" (rapidly shortened to ABIs)… seen as the answer to the geography of disadvantage'* (Smith *et al.*, 2007: 143). Education policy strands invoking community connection included Education Action Zones (EAZs), Excellence in Cities (EIC), Beacon Schools and Specialist Schools, Leadership Incentive Grants, the Leading Edge Partnership Programme, Networked Learning Communities and 14–19 Pathfinders. These were substantially funded national initiatives which purposefully required or encouraged schools to collaborate with other schools and often with other kinds of partners. The same government's 'Every Child Matters' and 'Extended Schools' policies included a commitment that, by 2010, children and families would be able to access a range of core services *'through schools located at the heart of the community'*. Schools were to be encouraged to create partnerships so that the offer could include:

- a varied range of activities including study support, sport and music clubs, combined with childcare in primary schools
- parenting and family support
- swift and easy access to targeted and specialist services
- community access to facilities including adult and family learning, ICT and sports grounds.

(DfES, 2005)

Since the change of national government in 2010, partnerships have continued to be an integral element in education discourse in England and generally, though not universally, held to be 'a good thing'. The National

College is promoting *'the need for new thinking'* about leadership models and partnerships and lists examples including federations, legal collaborations, Trusts, co-locations with other services, chains of schools and various combinations of those (NCSL, 2010). It has published a think piece by David Hargreaves arguing that a sustainable, self-improving school system requires the development of school clusters, local solutions, co-construction and 'system leaders' (Hargreaves, 2010). There is further scope for schools to develop their partnership roles with other schools and communities under the 2010 Coalition Government's 'Big Society' proposal for people and communities to be *'given more power and take more responsibility'* (Cabinet Office, 2010). Some schools may use their increasing autonomy to retreat from the extended concept into a narrower focus on academic attainment; others will use it to build broader alliances with their local community and other services.

Despite the general trends, individual school leaders have continued to position their schools as community hubs even when the systemic emphasis moved on to individualism and competition. We have written about some of those schools in other contexts (Mongon, 2010; Leadbeater, 2008). We now need to explain why their experience and the experiences of the schools reported later in this work are important to us.

Themes for a future story

We wrote above that not everything about the nationalisation and centralisation of the public education service in England has been misjudged or damaging. Some features of that trend have challenged or even overcome unhelpful aspects of professional hegemony and political obscurity. School leadership is in many ways improved, the quality of teaching is generally better and attainment outcomes for young people are higher. On the other hand, the impact of that approach appears to have run out of steam and the established narrative is no longer compelling for four reasons:

- improvements in educational attainments hit a plateau after early gains at the start of this century
- improved educational performance seems to have done little to reduce social and economic inequality
- a debate has been started about what education should be for at a time of rapid social, economic and technological changes
- there are increasing doubts about the effectiveness or sustainability of models of centralised, target-driven system improvement.

We could add a fifth reason: the concerns expressed by school leaders in a wide variety of settings that important aspects of their work outside the core of teaching and learning are not recognised publicly. Arrangements for reporting outcomes and processes for accountability have not properly acknowledged the contribution made by schools in actively engaging the wider community in shared support for children and young people. Leaders claim that this underestimated work, supporting the development of local role models and family learning and developing community networks by working collaboratively, is not just a contribution to pupil attainment. In some contexts it is essential if improvement is to take place. They also claim that the work has intrinsic value beyond attainment when it contributes to improved well-being for children and adults across localities through, for example, improved employment and reductions in anti-social behaviour. All of this, say these leaders, is an undervalued, neglected and, sometimes, even demeaned part of their effort.

Our challenge and that of sympathetic school leaders has been to present this undervalued work so it can be understood by a wide audience. If the work is important we should be able to describe it, identify its outcomes, assess its impact on core learning and celebrate successful examples. Policy makers, even some school leaders and parts of the wider community, do not necessarily understand what leaders committed to these approaches are trying to do or what the consequences are. If practitioners and researchers cannot tell the story together, how can anyone begin to appreciate its value? In the following chapters we will draw on the experience of the schools and leaders in the public value enquiry to illustrate some of the key threads which we believe can be themes in future leadership and in policy development.

Chapter 4

New authorisation

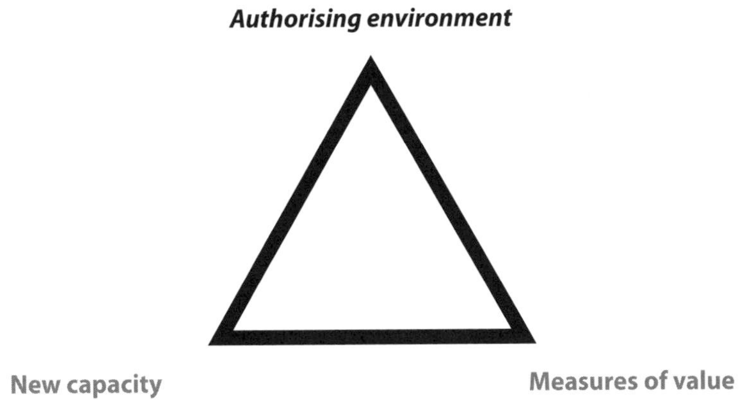

Authorising environment

New capacity

Measures of value

Figure 4.1: The authorising environment in the 'public innovation triangle'.

Source: Based on Moore (1995). Used by permission.

In the previous chapter, we made passing reference to five kinds of authorising environment on which school leaders are more or less dependent:

- Personal
- Associate
- Institutional
- Contextual
- National

In this chapter we will describe how the PV school leaders engaged with and contributed to the creation of different forms of authorising environment. In Chapters 5 and 6 we will explore how different authorising environments, in particular those conferring personal, associate and contextual authorisation, relate to the other two dimensions of the innovation triangle – *capacity* and *measures* – in the work of schools. In each of these three chapters we will refer to what have been called 'intelligences' – for which other appropriate labels might be disposition, capacity or literacy (Southworth, 2004). The label intelligence was adopted in an earlier work simply to capture the idea of a property of the mind which embraces several insights and abilities (Mongon and Chapman, 2008: 7–10). The three intelligences proposed in that earlier work – social, professional and contextual – seem to contribute correspondingly, though not exclusively, to the creation of personal, associate and contextual authorising environments.

Most of what needs to be said about the detail of institutional and national authorisation was covered in Chapter 3. Both have been the subject of burgeoning statutory definition through which the national authorisation has been increasingly centralised and the institutional increasingly specified. A striking feature of innovative activity and public value is how it is inserted into the spaces across and between nationally and institutionally circumscribed environments. Nonetheless, institutional authorisation, in effect the work of school governors, can enthuse or inhibit the impetus to create partnerships and public value: without other forms of authorisation, the buck stops with the school governors. 'In the absence of formal governance arrangements, responsibility for supporting the governance of partnerships falls to partners' own corporate governance mechanisms' (Audit Commission, 2005: 62).

To encourage support rather than opposition, PV leaders work with and on their statutory, institutional governing bodies to ensure that they too authorise the wider issues – beyond the core of teaching and learning – in which the leaders want the school to engage.

The PV school leaders are not neutral about the forms of authorisation, and therefore governance, which they believe are appropriate to their work: arguably, they neither could nor should be. The relationships between governance and executive roles in public service are necessarily and inevitably reciprocal (Feldman and Khademian, 2002). These relationships – between politicians, managers (of whom school leaders would be an example), other employees and the public – are too complex and varied to be explained by linear, mechanical and hierarchical models of control. Feldman and Khademian conclude 'that public managers play a role in the way these relationships are enacted and the structures that evolve. Influence over relationship structures in other words is reciprocal… And hence relationship structures can and do change' (ibid., 548).

In effect, the administration and management of public services is an undeniably political activity: even a decision to behave 'apolitically' will always have political consequences. Managing the relationship between political, authorising and executive activities has been a key function of the PV leaders.

Symmetric and asymmetric authorisation

The work which the PV leaders shared with us over the course of the National College sponsored enquiry has allowed us to draw some generalisations, which we can portray as theoretical constructs grounded in practice. That approach should allow the learning from the enquiry to be shared with, tested and challenged in other operational or research contexts. Table 4.1 suggests a model for thinking about two dimensions of authorisation we encountered – asymmetric and associate.

Table 4.1: Asymmetric and associate authorisation

	ASYMMETRIC AUTHORISATION	ASSOCIATE AUTHORISATION
SOURCE	PREFABRICATED	CULTIVATED
FRAMEWORK	LEGAL	ETHICAL
AUTHORITY	BASED ON POSITION	BASED ON TRUST

Source: Based on Mongon and Chapman (2012, Table 2.1)

- *Asymmetric authorisation* is *prefabricated* by powerful external agencies for use by the individuals and communities which constitute a public service and its users. Statutory requirements from national government or leverage from other high status institutions, the local authority for example, fall into this category. The legally constrained elements of a school governing body might also be in this category – depending on how they are carried out. *The framework* for asymmetric authorisation is predominantly legal and the authorised activity is therefore based on techno-legal relationships. *Position defines authority*: specific posts and appointments are associated with power and control.
- *Associate authorisation* is held together by common interest which, in turn, is defined and *cultivated* by the participating actors – providers, users and, when they are not in the other two groups, stakeholders. *The framework* is predominantly ethical; activity is based on expectations of 'the kind of people we are'. *Trust underpins authority*: hierarchical assumptions are challenged.

The PV school leaders, like others doing similar work, expect and generally accept an element of asymmetric authorisation inside the education service. They recognise the legitimacy of national and local government interest even when its particular expression does not feel instinctively compatible with their own perspectives. Associate authorisation is not a phrase they would choose to describe what they are doing; however, they are drawn both intuitively and professionally towards it. If they were theoreticians as well as expert practitioners, the PV school leaders might recognise their preference for associate authorisation as a preference for a variation on *'new public service theory'*. They might even explain their preference for those two in terms of their doubts about 'principal agent theory' and 'new public management theory' (Blaug et al., 2006: 10).

- The assumption behind 'principal agent theory' is that politicians will legislate for static, hierarchical and bureaucratic governance structures and hold managers accountable for mandated results.
- The assumption underpinning 'new public management theory' is that public sector organisations will emulate the entrepreneurial responsiveness of the private sector counterparts. Governance structures are the product of competition and compromise.
- The assumption informing 'new public service theory' is that public managers will help to build a collective, shared notion of the public interest, not merely aggregate and respond to individual preferences. In the 'new public service':

policies and programmes that effectively meet public needs are to be achieved through collective and collaborative processes that emphasise the importance of citizens over customers and people over productivity. Accountability requires that public managers respond to statutory and constitutional law, community values, political norms, professional standards and citizen interests.

(ibid.)

The principles behind these approaches can be tabulated for comparison. The broad trends in each of the three columns in Table 4.2 will be recognisable to anyone who has recently been working in the public education service in England. Even if there are few instances where a public service perfectly matches the archetype in each column and instead embraces elements of two or even three, the broad definitions will certainly be familiar.

Table 4.2: Comparing perspectives – public administration, public management and new public service

	Principal agent model	New public management model	New public service model
The public interest	Politically defined and expressed in law	Represents an aggregation of individual interests	Results from a dialogue about shared values
User–provider relationship	Clients and constituents	Customers	Citizens
Role of central and local government	Navigating: designing and implementing policies focusing on politically defined objectives	Steering: acting as a catalyst to facilitate market forces	Serving: brokering interests and creating shared values

	Principal agent model	New public management model	New public service model
Mechanisms for achieving policy objectives	Programmes administered through existing government agencies	Incentivising policy objectives through private and non-profit agencies	Building coalitions of public, non-profit and private agencies to meet mutually agreed needs
Approach to accountability	Hierarchical – administrators are responsible to elected politicians, in turn periodically accountable to an electorate	Market-driven – the accumulation of self-interest produces desired outcomes	Multi-faceted – public servants attend to the law, community values, political norms, professional standards and citizen interests
Assumed organisational structure	Bureaucracy marked by top-down authority and control or regulation of clients	Decentralised public organisations with primary control remaining with the agency	Collaborative structures with leadership shared internally and externally
Predominant motivation for public servants	Pay and benefits, civil service protection	Entrepreneurial spirit, ideological desire to reduce size of government	Public service, desire to contribute to society

Source: Based on Denhardt and Denhardt (2000: 554). Reproduced by permission.

Associate authorising environments are more likely to be found in contexts and institutions in which the operating principles are aligned with 'new public service theory'. In broad terms and drawing on Feldman and Khademian's typology (2002: 545), these are more likely to be authorising environments which tend to have:

- multiple, interlinking governance processes created through interactions of people in many different roles
- reciprocal arrangements in which a wide range of actors – including school leaders and other public managers – influence the structure of relationships that constitute governance structures and so constrain and enable one another's actions
- relatively dynamic rather than static features which provide opportunities for different actions, processes and structures to develop from each interaction
- evaluation based not only on targeted outcomes for users but also on the addition of public value and the promotion of democratic process
- accountability based on the visible and continuous assessment of results alongside a consideration of the appropriateness of the nature and quality of the relationships.

Practice behind the theory!

So how do the PV leaders locate themselves along the right hand column of Table 4.2 in order to develop new public service models, to nurture authorising environments and to promote public value?

> *Where public value takes you is beyond the school gates... and when that happens you have to exert more and more leadership... and lose more and more control. You are no longer in charge of what goes on out there. This is different to how you normally operate. On your own site, you manage things and provide leadership to what is a captive audience. With the public value approach you have minimal control of day to day management, but you have a key role in providing leadership to influence the agenda. You are with people who don't have the same professional background as you; who have different perspectives and possibly different motives to you. But what you do have in common is serving families and communities and that's the bedrock to your leadership. Influencing becomes a major part of your leadership toolkit.*
> Margaret Nowell, Headteacher, St Thomas's Centre Pupil Referral Unit

The relationship between a school and its wider community is both a very simple and a very complex matter. It is a relationship that embraces some hard practical features and some contested philosophical concepts. Practically, the school sits in a particular location, offering services to the young people and families there. Often, the location will be narrowly defined within limited neighbourhood boundaries although sometimes it will have a broader meaning when a school's community is more widespread, for example in thinly populated areas and in special schools whether with quite narrow or relatively wide boundaries. Philosophically, this relationship raises profound questions for the PV leaders about what the service should be and how it should be delivered, including: 'who is the school for?', 'who owns it?' and 'what is its community?' The answers the PV leaders shared with us are summarised both in broad terms and with some specific examples below.

Who is our school for?

> *We want to extend our work to include families who may not access the Children's Centre by working with parents to jointly develop parent and children's groups in the community centres, rather than at our base. We want to develop capacity by encouraging peer support so that families are able to provide support themselves and to each other. We want to engage other services so that families experience a joined up provision rather than see us all as separate entities.*
> Kathy Stevens, Head of Centre, Castle Children's Centre and Nursery School

PV leaders tend to describe the school as primarily for the pupils – and then for anyone whose learning and well-being can benefit from working together. There are potentially no limits to that definition except the constraints of imagination and energy. We shall report later that the PV leaders never lose sight of the importance of attainment for their pupils and therefore of the focus on a high quality adult contribution. They understand how much that depends on the continued learning of the staff, repeatedly identified as a central factor in school effectiveness (Day *et al.*, 2008a, Robinson *et al.*, 2009). They also recognise *'...that schools are one of the few public institutions with both the capacity and the opportunity to generate social capital within the communities that they serve'* (Flint 2010: 4). This leads them to encourage parental engagement and learning in a variety of imaginative ways to which we will return later.

Who owns our school?

> *To develop effective provision we need to be clear what the needs of our differing communities are. This has involved us undertaking extensive consultation exercises and talking and listening to what people want. We also have to be aware that we complement existing provision and that we work co-operatively with other providers rather than in direct competition.*
> Jo Grail, formerly Headteacher, Delaware Community Primary School

To PV leaders 'ownership' is not a technical matter determined by statutory definitions of institutional status. It is an ethical matter more closely connected to responsibility and accountability. These school leaders are prepared to be *responsible* for a wide range of attainment and other outcomes. They also accept that they should be *accountable*: that a range of individuals and organisations outside the school have the right to have information so they can scrutinise and comment on their work. They therefore create processes alongside and beyond the statutory governance requirements to make the school accountable in different ways to different groups, including government, governors, pupils, families, staff, other schools and services and the neighbourhood.

What is our community?

- *To advance and enhance the development and education of people of all ages and without distinction*
- *To advance the health and welfare of pupils and their families*
- *To promote community cohesion*
- *To provide or assist in providing facilities for recreation and leisure time activities at all times of the year*

- *To work with schools in challenging circumstances with the purpose of developing long term sustainable relationships for the benefit of children and families within the local community*
  Objectives of the Garforth School Partnership Trust

An insight into the PV leaders' sense of community crystallised during a parallel enquiry into schools which had contributed successfully to community cohesion (Mongon, 2010). The interviewed leaders, like those in this enquiry, littered their conversations and accounts with the word 'community'. Their membership of three interlinked communities, each with its own subsidiaries, was evidently a significant lens through which they looked at their work.

1. *The school community:* a place where everyone is a learner and contributes to the learning of others.
2. *The neighbourhood community:* a locality within which adults can be offered learning opportunities and can contribute to the learning of their children.
3. *The provider community:* the network of voluntary and statutory services whose members can learn from one another and contribute to one another's learning.

Like those leaders, PV leaders are clear about what it meant to be a member of each of those communities and to be one leader amongst many leaders, inside as well as outside their schools. They promote parity of status and a commitment to shared learning in the school, neighbourhood and provider communities. The school is a community in its own right; it also contains distinctive professional and student communities, is part of a wider community of children's services, is inside the community that lives or works around us, and it includes widespread faith and neighbourhood communities whose children are on roll. The school's community therefore includes all the internal and external groups with which it wants to associate itself and vice versa.

Three authorising environments

Personal authorisation

You must have confidence in yourself and trust in others…
Dave Dunkley, Headteacher Coleshill Heath Primary School

In Chapter 3, we made a passing reference to *personal authorisation,* writing that it is based to a large degree on each leader's own dispositions – the permissions they give and demands they make on themselves. Personal authorisation becomes increasingly important when a system becomes characterised by institutional autonomy as, arguably, England's is now. With increasing institutional autonomy comes increasing opportunity for the full-time professional executives to exert influence on their institutions and their mainly part-time governance arrangements. Michael Gove, Secretary of State for Education in England, told the 2011 Education World Forum:

> *[With] headteachers and principals free to determine how pupils are taught and how budgets are spent, the greater the potential there has been for all-round improvement and the greater the opportunity too for the system to move from good to great… [providing] an opportunity to thrive, free from interference from government… making schools more accountable to their communities…*
>
> (Gove, 2011)

To create their own sense of personal authorisation PV leaders appear to draw on what has been described as *social intelligence*. This phrase was coined in an earlier work about school leaders who are effective in adverse circumstances (Mongon and Chapman, 2008: 9). The PV leaders, like the earlier group, appear to have a high level of personal skills rooted in and demonstrated by their obvious respect for the people around them – irrespective of age or status. It is an attitude which generates powerful reciprocity. It is an approach rooted in a value system with a belief about how people should behave towards one another. Their colleagues believe that these leaders are uncompromising in their protection of the school's values and practices. As a result they can create an atmosphere in which high expectations are seen as evidence of care and concern and not as surveillance or constraint.

In the same earlier work, attention was drawn to three key characteristics of effective leaders: in broad terms – self-confidence, personal responsibility and conscientiousness. These are also common to the PV leaders and central to understanding each leader's personal authorising environment.

- **Self-confidence** is a recurring characteristic of leaders in the literature on school improvement and effectiveness. The accompanying belief in personal capability and capacity authorises the leader to tackle difficult tasks, to take risks and to persist if success is not immediate or even in the face of initial failure. Persistence and eventual success create learned behaviour, reinforcing the original confidence. Day's comprehensive review of the literature noted that in both primary and secondary sectors, heads from more disadvantaged schools appeared to have more positive views about their 'self-efficacy'. The majority of key staff also viewed their head teachers similarly – all of which Day concluded was *'arguably a very good thing given the scope of the challenges they face'* (Day *et al.*, 2008b: xvi).
- **Personal responsibility** 'authorises' leaders to examine the outcomes of their work critically and to test rigorously whether

they are personally satisfied with the results. Leaders with this characteristic tend to attribute events in their life to their own control. They are not inclined to blame anyone else for the school's problems and are inclined to see the destiny of the school as in its own hands, individually and collectively accepting responsibility for its difficulties and claiming credit for its triumphs. They feel they should control the variables that are at their disposal and are prepared to be accountable for that.

- **Conscientiousness** authorises these leaders *'to be contentious and to deal with conflict, highly pragmatic, resilient and determined'* (Harris and Chapman, 2002: 3). They feel permitted, perhaps even obliged, to face up to making difficult decisions and have *'a passion for order and thoroughness…an insistence, persistence and consistency about certain non-negotiables'* (DfES, 2007: 11). Conscientious individuals tend to be painstaking, self-disciplined, organised, careful before acting and people who are striving to achieve. The ambition and sense of perfection with which these leaders are sometimes struggling appears to contribute as much to the quality of the relationships they create around them as to student outcomes.

The PV leaders in the National College's enquiry were encouraged to spend some time sharing information and ideas about their personal authorisation and together agreed that the following eight dimensions, in no particular order, informed what they are trying to do.

1. **Having high expectations *for* as well as *with* children and families**
    Successful leaders for public value are centred on establishing what works best for children, young people and their families. They understand that families and neighbourhoods hold the key to unlocking the potential of young people. They also know that raising the aspirations of children alone is insufficient to effect lasting change. So they create public value by sharing responsibility *with and for* adults in the wider community. Because they also believe in community ownership of solutions, they facilitate and encourage a self-help approach that builds social capacity and sustainability. Finally, they know that young people are agents of change and not passive participants, so they increase the engagement and participation of young people.

2. **Having clear vision and focus: a long-term strategy that builds resilience into the system**
    Successful leaders for public value have a clear vision of how their work will bring about the changes that are needed for lasting

improvement. They have what has been called a 'living vision', the antithesis of platitude, a driver for action which needs to be:

- *focused*, creating an invigorating sense of purpose and courage
- *feasible*, fuelling people with energy, passion and enjoyment
- *desirable*, offering an ending worth going for
- *imaginable*, enabling all the stakeholders to answer the question: 'what is it?'

(Innovation Unit, 2009)

There may be a need for tactical quick fixes along the way but the longer-term strategy is crucial: a vision of community regeneration centred on children and young people. These leaders believe that nothing need be insurmountable but they acknowledge that improving outcomes isn't always easy and that determined action is needed, particularly where there are thorny and entrenched issues.

3. **Nothing needs to be insurmountable, but risks will have to be taken**

   Successful leaders for public value have an optimistic view about the challenges, together with a belief that effective work to improve outcomes does not happen in neat silos. They are ambitious for their communities and are willing to translate this ambition into radical approaches and solutions. Doing more of the same is not an option for them and an absence of blueprints is not daunting, rather it encourages creative activity and a 'let's sort this together' approach.

4. **Harnessing all the drivers: school improvement is the foundation but seize the other initiatives too**

   Successful leaders for public value use the hooks and drivers that enable them to join up the complex agendas including health, well-being, community cohesion, regeneration and social responsibility. They understand that the issues facing communities are multi-faceted and require a joined-up approach, so they move in and out of agendas and funding streams in order to maximise the resource available. These leaders have 'sticky fingers' and are able to access bids and funding to further their work in the community. They are not precious about where they get ideas from. *'Innovators are inveterate borrowers. The best way to have a new idea is to mix together two existing ideas to create a new blend'* (Leadbeater 2012: 92).

5. **Using opportunities and skills to best effect, including multi-agency working, to bring consistency for families through shared systems and processes**

   Successful leaders for public value recognise the interdependency of agencies in providing the best service for families and communities. They understand that professional background is of little concern to families: it is the family's experience of the quality and the effectiveness of the connection or intervention that matters. Crucially, these leaders recognise that the entrenched issues facing some communities will only be addressed by working on the solutions together. They find themselves providing strategic direction for workers from a variety of professional backgrounds. They understand the importance of professional expertise but they challenge the idea of preciousness.

6. **Having total transparency – building trust and consulting appropriately with families and community as well as staff and other providers**

   Successful leaders for public value work purposefully to develop trust with the community and between the agencies who serve it. Consultation builds on this notion of trust – not the kind that just pays lip service when decisions have already been determined, but the kind that genuinely requires children, families and wider communities to express their views. In the jargon of the day, they are ethnographers, participant researchers, close enough to a community to paint an intimate portrait.

7. **Making time to plan, reflect and seek inspiration: self-development**

   Successful leaders for public value recognise the need for time to plan and reflect. There are no handbooks or blueprints for this work, so reflection is even more critical for developing ways forward. In the absence of detailed guidance the leaders point to the need for inspiration to refresh the energies and to encourage risk taking. Self-development is a characteristic often associated with effective leaders of change but it is not always easy to pin down in the more informal and *ad hoc* activity of leadership for public value.

8. **Having self-belief and passion, resilience and single mindedness, nurturing relationships and being positively 'can do'**

   Successful leaders for public value understand that the attitude of the leaders within the organisation is critical to the success of their approach – and this doesn't apply exclusively to the senior team. Much can be achieved by encouraging enterprise and creativity lower down the organisation. These leaders share the view that momentum is unstoppable when embraced by enthusiasts at grass roots level.

Associate authorisation

In Chapter 3 we introduced a passing reference to *associate authorisation*, noting that it depends on the bonding which PV leaders create between themselves, the adults and the children who are working together daily. The adjective 'associate' is used to capture the sense of association – the potential of a school as a community of partners or companions assembled for a common purpose. This is close to what Fielding describes as *'radical collegiality'* (1999) or a *'dialogic form of democratic practice'* (2001: 130). Radical collegiality, Fielding points out, is not the same as radical collaboration and rests on the necessity of the shared endeavour being informed by the ethics and ideals of teaching and education, not just the mutual exchange of information and skills (2006: 311). In other words *'…the nature of teaching in schools is such that a professionalism adequate to our needs in the twenty-first century must incorporate a much more overt openness and reciprocity indicative of a much more flexible, dialogic form of democratic practice'* (2001: 130).

Because PV leaders know and understand that a community with a shared sense of endeavour will be a stronger community, they work hard to explain their actions to staff and students, to canvass their opinions and to gain their communal authorisation. This approach is more profound and complex than the distributed leadership which has been *'the leadership idea of the moment'* (Harris and Spillane 2008: 13). Their approach is closer to what MacBeath calls symbiosis: *'While delegation is expressed in "giving" responsibility to others or allowing responsibility by structural default, symbiosis has a more organic quality'* (MacBeath, 2008: 53). Readers may have encountered similar approaches described as creating what Szreter called *'bridging capital'* in contrast to *'bonding capital'* : *'bridging social capital is characterized by many and weak links, a fluidity of relationships which is always alive to something new and challenging. In open, boundary-less relationships, leadership moves fluidly and un-self-consciously among people'* (Szreter, 2004: 52).

The PV leaders will occasionally adopt tactics from the personality-based or techno-managerial handbooks of school leadership if needs must but tend to believe that no amount of charismatic leadership or target-driven effort can provide sustainable, positive development for an organisation. Their inclination towards associate authorisation presumes that leadership is a phenomenon which inevitably permeates an organisation. Everyone in the school has a hand in leadership by default and so in its endemic forms leadership will be exercised either in support of the agreed aims or to undermine them. These leaders work to ensure that leadership in all its forms is transparent across the organisation and that part of the leadership role shared by every member is to provide a critical though supportive authorising environment. We will see this approach repeated in the next chapter when we consider how the PV leaders increasingly move their leadership and influence further outside the official boundaries of the school. As a broad rule of thumb, the more settled the school becomes or as networks are created further beyond the school, the less dominant are the managerial aspects of the leaders' interactions and the more dominant are the leadership elements. This requires leaders to be purposeful about letting go of detail that cannot be controlled – a tactic that may feel counter-intuitive for some people with a background in classroom teaching and a career in the recent target-driven development of school leadership. This *'purposeful letting go'*, as one of the PV leaders described it, is balanced by the very close attention that the leaders then give to the remaining selected priority areas.

We referred in the previous section to the social intelligence which PV leaders seem to use in pursuit of personal authorisation. Professional Intelligence is the equivalent attribute in creating associate authorisation. These leaders are very good at their core business: leadership and management which nurture excellent standards of teaching and learning. Like all effective leaders, they have an acute sense of what is happening across the school. They modulate leadership and management at different times to match the development stages of the schools and will adopt tight central control when circumstances appear to demand it. At the same time, they are constantly seeking to move in the direction of the distributed, endemic leadership which will provide associate authorisation. Staff and students are clear about their own accountabilities and are encouraged to take personal responsibility for their own achievement and to share responsibility for communal outcomes, rather than superficially subscribing to rules which they might then persistently undermine. Disciplined risk taking is also encouraged and occasional misjudgements are tolerated on the understanding that the consequent learning and development are exploited.

This leads to organisations which have a *'learning orientation'* rather than a *'performance orientation'* a commitment to *'improving'* rather than *'proving'* (Watkins *et al.*, 2007: 46). This is what Copland's study of the Bay Area School Reform Collaborative (BASRC) in San Francisco describes as an emphasis on collective activity, focused on collective goals, spanning traditional organisational roles and based on expertise rather than hierarchical authority, to *'communities of practice built around cycles of enquiry'* (Copland, 2003: 379).

Contextual authorisation

Remember your social responsibility as a leader. It is your duty to consider what you can do to support the community so that it can begin to thrive, and then support itself. You need your staff to understand that they are serving the community, not the other way around.

Sheila Audsley, former Headteacher, Clifton Green Primary School

In Chapter 3, we made a passing reference to contextual authorisation, writing that it is created when school leaders expand their sphere of influence into the neighbourhood and professional communities around their school. In the absence of legally determined formulae for the governance of collaborative activity, the PV leaders created *ad hoc*, fit-for-purpose arrangements. Contextual authorisation emerges in the cracks where neither institutional authorisation nor national authorisation have permeated. Governance is the statutory and institutional expression of the authorising environments which provide the accountability framework for professional work. For schools, this is still legally vested in the governing body. The formal governance of some other aspects of work through which schools might promote public value is with the local authority, the local children's trust or some of the area arrangements they have created as we shall see in Chapters 5 and 6. There are still other parts of the work that fall outside any formal arrangements and which therefore become both a conceptual challenge in terms of identifying who has authority and accountability – either moral or technical – as well as a practical opportunity for creating new and strong community and service alliances. It is in those parts that contextual authorisation emerges.

We referred in the preceding sections to the professional and social intelligence which are characteristics of PV and other effective leaders. Contextual Intelligence is the equivalent attribute in creating contextual authorisation. PV leaders have a profound respect for the context they are working in and resist patronising it. They are sensitive to local issues without being condescending. They prefer to talk about the strengths of the local community rather than its weaknesses, approaching it as a potential resource rather than an inevitable obstacle. They see advantages in integrated approaches to the needs of young people – though not necessarily in integrated service structures. They believe the school can contribute to a variety of outcomes for young people including, though not exclusively, academic attainment. The corollary is that others can contribute in turn to the school's core activity, teaching and learning. They have a 360 degree view of their position in a range of local networks as well as in the local and national political environments.

So what is the context from which the PV leaders sourced their contextual authorisation? To illustrate its complexity, we want to draw an analogy between headship and being the chief executive of a small to medium-sized company. The latter will not be a simple posting but would have a limited production range, accountability to a board of directors and management of a work force of dozens. In its simplest forms it has the advantages of clarity around purpose, scope and scale. Something similar might be said about the role of a headteacher responsible to a governing body for the quality of teaching and learning in a school and for levels of pupil attainment – not necessarily an easy role but one that is set within a fairly clear framework of expectations and accountability. The game changes when either moves beyond the core business.

Companies that move beyond the relatively tightly defined activities which create their core service or product generally do so because they want to influence the quality and dependability of their raw material supplies or to influence how well their products perform in the market place. They might therefore take control of their suppliers and outlets. They might create a centrally managed chain of command along the line of supply, production and sales. This kind of 'command control' is not the only option for ensuring security and quality along that line. For a variety of reasons, private sector companies are increasingly exploring the potential of more equitable and empowering relationships with their chain of suppliers and customers to provide their businesses with the confidence they need.

Schools that want to affect the lives of their children and families directly so that their learning can be improved and who want to contribute to improving pupils' adult life chances by enhancing the local community, do not have the option of creating a centrally managed chain of command across the contributing elements. Few would want that option. They can, however, imitate the option of creating a series of collaborations and alliances with varying patterns of authority, power and influence across the institutions, organisations and communities on which children and young people depend. It is axiomatic that the further schools move from the core of teaching and learning on a single school site, the more adaptive their leadership and governance arrangements need to be.

The complexity of the role as it moves from core to extensive is elegantly illustrated in 'pictures' shared with the enquiry group by two of the school leaders. In the first, Jo Grail, then headteacher at Delaware Community Primary School, now Director of Leadership Development at the Learning Institute, shared her mind map of activity as the lead professional for a school, as a partner in the provision of extended services and as a contributor to community cohesion (map reproduced with her permission in Figure 4.2). Following this is the diagram shared by Coleshill Heath Primary School and designed by the North Solihull Extended Services team to illustrate 'supervisory' relationships (Figure 4.3). We have added a column at the right-hand edge of the original North Solihull diagram to illustrate how new relationships might emerge as a school becomes involved, for example, in Children's Trust arrangements or community partnerships.

Figure 4.3 reveals the complexity of leadership and management in extensive settings. Its two axes represent two dimensions of leadership and management: 'formal <> informal' and 'ad hoc <> planned'. In each of the cells, leaders exercise an educative (E), managerial (M) or supportive (S) role broadly analogous, respectively, to a coaching, management and mentoring role. The weighting of the roles differs between cells and the model signals which are the dominant (though not exclusive) roles in each using the initials E, M or S.

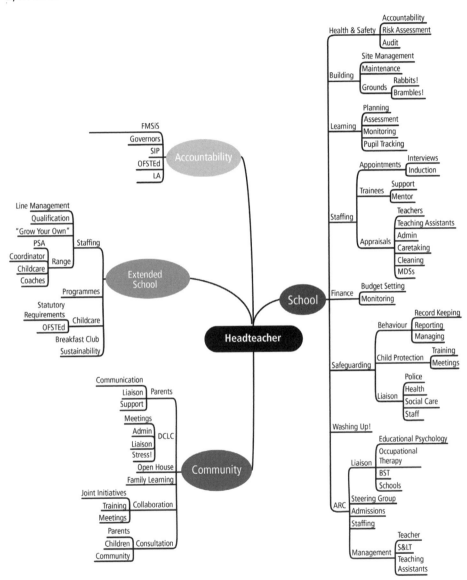

Figure 4.2: A headteacher's mind map as lead professional for a school, a partner of extended services provision and a contributor to community cohesion.

Reproduced with the permission of Jo Grail, formerly headteacher, Delaware Community Primary School

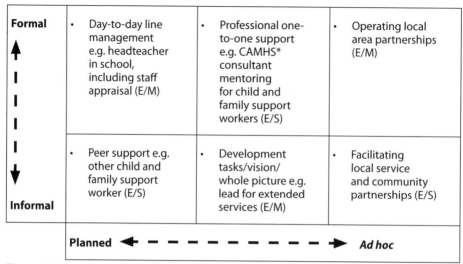

Formal ↑	• Day-to-day line management e.g. headteacher in school, including staff appraisal (E/M)	• Professional one-to-one support e.g. CAMHS* consultant mentoring for child and family support workers (E/S)	• Operating local area partnerships (E/M)
↓ **Informal**	• Peer support e.g. other child and family support worker (E/S)	• Development tasks/vision/ whole picture e.g. lead for extended services (E/M)	• Facilitating local service and community partnerships (E/S)

Planned ← – – – – – – – – → **Ad hoc**

Figure 4.3: Locality relationships model

Initials for educative (E), managerial (M) or supportive (S) signal the dominant roles

* Child and Adolescent Mental Health Services

Source: Payne and Shand, 2009; adapted from Payne and Scott (1982). Used by permission.

Jo Grail's mind map (figure 4.2, previous page) shows how, even within school, the leadership role is already complex and extends beyond the core of teaching and learning. Outside school the role encounters various organisations of external accountability, delivers or co-creates extended services and engages with a wider set of community issues. All these, should only be taking the leader's time if they are also contributing, more or less directly, to better outcomes for young people. The North Solihull model (Figure 4.3) shows how the role taken by school leaders becomes less formal and planned, and more informal and *ad hoc*, as the service and professional relationship become less directly connected to that core classroom activity. In the bottom right-hand box, for example, school leaders can no longer fall back on the formal authority of their position. Their management capacity at that point is minimal or non-existent. They are drawn into behaviour which places great emphasis on skills of negotiation and on attitudes of equal respect and esteem. They are dependent on contextual authorisation and their leadership has become what Close and Wainwright (2010) call cultural, increasingly dependent on facilitation, coaching, analysis, vision, story-telling, advocacy and negotiation. The contextual authorising environments allow PV leaders and those they are working with to resolve seven dilemmas which can be generated by contextual partnership activity.

• *Structural dilemmas*: in which schools are often metaphorically isolated by their habits and literally isolated by their campus walls.

- *Ideological dilemmas*: in which schools may be seen by others as having marginalised issues of equity and social justice in pursuit of limited targets.
- *Procedural dilemmas*: in which the apparently implacable rhythms of the timetable, school day and academic terms figure, are considerable features.
- *Inter-professional dilemmas*: in which views about status and hierarchy figure largely.
- *Human resource dilemmas*: in which the varying conditions of service between salaried groups, not all entitled to a long summer break, create tensions.
- *Political dilemmas*: in which the different lines of accountability for different targets create potentially contradictory assumptions about priorities and practices.
- *Symbolic dilemmas:* in which the use of common terms to mean different things across professional groups can be particularly confusing.

(Based on Close and Wainwright 2010: 443–6.)

In the next chapter we will report on how the PV leaders created capacity to support the innovations which in turn promoted public value. We will define five types of capacity ranging from the core of teaching and learning through to social capital with only indirect, if any, impact in classrooms. It will become apparent that authorisation for the tasks follows the North Solihull model from formal to informal and from planned to *ad hoc*. That, in turn, is reflected in the governance arrangements to which we now turn.

Visible authorisation – creating governance

The need to establish contextual authorisation led the public value leaders into a variety of governance arrangements – though governance is not always the word they used to describe the activities reported upon in this section. For the purposes of the enquiry, we defined governance as:

> the visible ways in which groups across the ten sites defined what they were going to do, how they were going to do it, where the authority to make decisions rested and, finally, how the completed work was approved.

What follows is a brief summary of the variety of arrangements.

All of the schools had a governing body and St Thomas's Centre Pupil Referral Unit and Castle Children's Centre each had management groups. These bodies set the organisation's vision, agreed statutory targets and reviewed performance within the familiar regulatory framework.

Two of the schools were building wider alliances across their communities at a higher, strategic level by becoming Trust Schools. The longer running of the two trust arrangements – at Garforth near Leeds – had created an alliance of trustees including the secondary school, four primary schools, the local further education college, the primary care trust and the Learning and Skills Council. Each of the schools retained its own governing body which focused on teaching and learning, while the Trust provided a vehicle for shared activity across children's services. It also provided the hub to share planning, facilities and provision to guarantee the core extended services offer to families across the locality. The Trust also sponsored local enterprise, including its own retail sites, to improve the personalised curriculum offer to young people.

George Green's Secondary School had exploited trust and not-for-profit approaches without becoming a Trust School. Stella Bailey, the school's director of extended services, is a trustee of the local Isle of Dogs Community Foundation – a voluntary charitable foundation responding to local needs and sponsoring a range of community activities in that corner of East London. The school had created Island Sports Trust (IST), another charitable, not-for-profit organisation, to facilitate and manage the community's use of the school's sports facilities. IST has eight trustees, is now an employer of mainly local residents and shows a small annual trading surplus. In contrast, the school adopted a more informal arrangement within the Docklands Youth Service (DYS) – a network of 20 youth service providers – which is the consortium backing the school's tender to provide the local youth service. The substantive contract is with the school while the DYS is one of the key guiding influences on the development of the youth work.

Wherever there were children's centres on PV school sites, the school governing bodies and the centre management committees were independent. The headteacher and chair of governors were often members of the children's centre management committee with a reciprocal arrangement in relation to the school governing body. Nationally, there are other governance models for schools and centres sharing a site, some of which make the centre management committee a sub-committee of the school governing body, sometimes with the headteacher as overall manager (Mongon et al. 2010).

These arrangements illustrate how schools can use statutory frameworks to assemble new designs for overseeing the alliances they want to make. On the whole though, the formal arrangements researched in this enquiry appeared to be populated by adults who were used to operating in committee environments. The arrangements were also mainly focused on pre-defined tasks such as running a school, centre, or youth service. Attempts by the schools to collaborate around less tightly defined issues, with adults who did not have experience of committee protocols, increased the complexity of governance and resulted in a turbulent experience of success and challenge.

Asking people drawn together with some spontaneity and enthusiasm around a common ambition to think about their governance arrangements before they do anything else would, in many cases, rip the heart out of the intention. Eventually, though, relationships come to the stage, sometimes driven by legal necessity or internal tension, when sustainability requires agreed clarity about the point of it all, about how decisions are made, who has what authority and whether things are going well. The more parties are in the relationship the more necessary and difficult reaching that clarity can become.

Sheila Audsley, then Headteacher at Clifton Green Primary School, provided an eloquent description of the uncertainties and insecurities around establishing community partnerships:

> The events turned out excellent... but it took a real leap of faith to get there... Who to invite? Where shall we host it? What if stakeholders can't agree? What happens if people kick off? What if everyone wants funding and we can't find it? What if they all look to me – because I'm the Head – for the answers on what to do?
>
> We held the first community partnership meeting sponsored by our school in the local community centre, off site deliberately and involving the key partners and stakeholders, obviously including parents. To create parity, the event was led by an external facilitator… We deliberately encouraged a cross section of parents including those who rarely engaged with school and other services. Three primary school and two secondary heads from the community came along with a range of services including health, social care, police, and representatives from the voluntary, faith and community sector: 50 plus people in a community hall with an interest in improving the life chances of children in the area – absolutely brilliant! All fears unfounded. I did have to influence, guide and provide direction, but I also had to listen and to learn from families and agencies who knew far more than me and who wanted to have a direct involvement in solving the issues raised, rather than being delivered to. I am now part of the steering group which guides this approach and I am learning leadership lessons every day.

The community learning committee at Delaware Community Primary School, the adventure playground group at Coleshill Heath Primary School and the steering groups emerging from the partnership at Clifton Green Primary School each did what it said on their tins – supported community learning, sponsored a community activity and facilitated community partnerships. Each of them was also an example of informal, though visible and secure, governance arrangements rising out of *ad hoc* networks. Arrangements like these are often sufficient for a short-term enterprise but tensions can emerge over time, not least when a highly motivated group is an alliance of disparate interests around a shared objective. Tensions most commonly come to the fore when the sustainability of the group is threatened or decisions are disputed. Paradoxically, tensions appear to thrive on the same ambiguity of rules and roles that generated a sense of partnership and mutual esteem in the first place. A partnership, for example, that has campaigned for new community premises might find it difficult to arbitrate between its members' different expectations about how the premises might be used, about how time and space might be allocated and how those decisions are made. In different circumstances, a campaigning set-up group might not accept responsibility for the maintenance of new provision. When the rules are not clear enough to resolve the contested decision making, the roles can become confused.

The PV leaders reported that, in difficult circumstances, their efforts to become a partner in the enterprise and to empower others to take on leading roles could be threatened by a default expectation that the headteacher would take the decisions, arbitrate and find the wherewithal to maintain the activity. Several of the leaders have needed to be resolute about resisting the expectation that partnership can revert to traditional hierarchies.

The PV leaders also believed in encouraging pupils and students – from early years to school leavers – to take responsibility for the life of their institutions. The school council at Coleshill Heath Primary School was used as the springboard for the local authority's consultation with pupils about school reorganisation proposals. The pupils' great hope after secondary transfer was that they would make new friends and their greatest fear was that their new classmates would be unfriendly. Clifton Green Primary School held school council meetings attended by pupils, staff and a governor. It also had a peer mediation scheme which involved a group of children looking and listening in the playground to help other children experiencing difficulties. At Garforth Community College, the school council has a 'manifesto' commitment to:

- improving facilities in school
- developing links with one of Leeds' twin cities – Durban in South Africa
- security in school
- ending bullying.

The school council has elected representatives to the Garforth and Swillington Community Forum, the Leeds Youth Council and the UK Youth Parliament.

Summary

The powerful threads running through these leaders' approaches to authorisation appear to be:

- **A strong sense of purpose** – these leaders have a clear set of priorities and goals which, nevertheless, they are prepared to subject to challenge and scrutiny.
- **A belief in capability** – these leaders think that they and their immediate team and wider partnership can make a difference to pupils' lives if the right work can be appropriately authorised and delivered.
- **A commitment to sharing** – these are leaders for whom the medium is the message: sharing responsibility and credit is what they strive to do with their pupils and staff and then with a wider network.
- **A construction of mutual trust** – these leaders engender trust from others and trust others, whatever their age or status, to make the best contribution they are allowed to make and promote authorising environments which support that.

Public value leaders place a high priority on creating contextual authorisation for their work. National authorisation creates the systemic grain along which they work, adapting the national warp and weave to local priorities as best they can. Institutional authorisation, derived from the school governing body, cannot be taken for granted. PV leaders are not passive about their relationship with school governors and work purposefully to align the governors' insights and ambitions alongside their professional judgements about the work to be done.

Personal and associate authorisation are fundamental aspects of the leaders' work with their schools. The first of these is, by definition, intuitive and the latter only slightly more cerebral. Together these two authorisations appear to sit at the heart of each leader's view of themselves and what they want to achieve professionally. For these leaders, how things are done cannot be separated from what needs to be done and what the outcomes should be.

Perhaps because of the focus of the enquiry and the questions we asked, contextual authorisation emerged as a central and demanding feature of innovative and public value activity. One way to think about the processes at work around these schools might be to see them as what Ainscow *et al.* (2012) call *'an ecology of equity'*. Students' experiences and outcomes are not dependent solely on what happens inside the school, they are affected by a wide range of other variables in demography, culture, employment, poverty and policy. PV leaders are not prepared to be passive about those factors. In part, they actively seek to mitigate some of the social and systemic inequities but they realise that the impact will be marginal. More important, perhaps, is the symbolic effect of their visible engagement with those issues – an engagement which nurtures loyalty and commitment from families as well as from other service providers. In the next chapter, we will describe how that reciprocity creates capacity for the school.

Chapter 5

Building new capacity

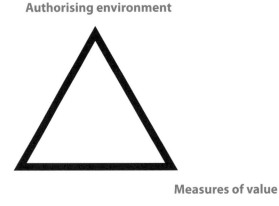

Authorising environment

New capacity   **Measures of value**

Figure 5.1: New capacity in the 'public innovation triangle'.

Source: Based on Moore (1995). Used by permission.

In Chapter 2 we proposed that innovation requires the development of authorising environments, *new capacity* and appropriate measures of value. In this chapter we consider new capacity in more detail and, in particular, report on how the PV leaders responded to that requirement.

The PV leaders, as we showed in the previous chapter, drew deeply on personal, associate and contextual authorisation for the permissions to drive their work in the directions they had chosen. They recognised the legitimacy of national and institutional authorisations and tolerated what they perceived as the limitations of those two. Their accommodation of those authorisations was reflected in their connection with the development of national and institutional capacity. They had no recognisable impact on the former and only marginal, though important, influence over the latter. In contrast, they had very significant impact on the development of new personal, associate and contextual capacity around their schools and localities. We will return shortly to those three more accessible forms of capacity but need first to make some reference to where institutional and national capacity *do* fit into the picture.

National capacity

National capacity has not been sensitive to variations in local circumstances and consequent need over the past quarter century or so. It has been hidebound by the combination of centralising legislation and national political management which we described in previous chapters. It is worth repeating however, that the cracks within and between these two provide the micro-ecology in which other forms of authorisation and capacity development can flourish. In national terms, the public value enquiry reported here extended over the last two years of the Labour Government; our analysis and writing coincided with the first 18 months of the Coalition Government. In broad terms, the PV leaders found their approach increasingly supported by aspects of the rhetoric and funding which expanded national capacity in the first decade of this millennium. That support was constrained by the continuing national emphasis on competition and a narrow range of outcome measures. The jury is out on the attitude of the Coalition Government to schools' engagement with community and social issues though, like its predecessor, the messages it gives are not obviously consistent. There is though a thread in right-of-centre analyses which suggests that this is a matter best left to local rather than to national determination. Writing under the banner of the Centre for Policy Studies, about the 60 programmes summarised in the Labour Government's 2007 'Children's Plan', Burkard and Clelford describe confidence in central regulation as misplaced, bureaucratic, ineffective, damaging and expensive.

> ...a more effective – and incidentally, far cheaper – alternative would be to devolve as much as possible, as far down as possible: responsibility for these initiatives should in most cases be passed to parents, to professionals, to schools and to local authorities.
>
> (Burkard and Clelford, 2010: 44)

Neither government, however, has appeared interested in, still less capable of, moving from 'technical innovation' to 'disruptive innovation'. In terms of the education innovation grid we introduced in Chapter 2 (Table 2.1), the national focus has been on IMPROVING and SUPPLEMENTING the current system. REINVENTION and TRANSFORMATION are not what centralised administrations easily understand or find comfortable. 'Disruptive innovation' is more likely to emerge deeper in or from the periphery of systems. It is an enormous challenge for politicians and administrators to identify and nurture the disruptive activity which has the potential to become constructive – in effect, to separate daft ideas which will make sense from the merely daft ideas. In healthy organisations, there are always plenty of both.

National capacity is determined in part by the resources which central government makes available for schools – including cash and qualified personnel – and in part by the encouragements its policy statements offer to school leaders by creating perceptions of what is acceptable activity. In that context, the use of nationally sponsored Area Based Initiatives (ABIs) to promote educational improvement runs back at least 40 years to the time of the Plowden Report (Plowden, 1967) and the introduction of Educational Priority Areas. More recently, over the past 12 years or so, there has been no lack of fiddling with national capacity through ABIs. Some of that fiddling has been of direct interest to school leaders who want to create public value (even if that is not what they would call it!). Some neighbourhood regeneration programmes promoted ABIs in which schools could be included but for which they were not central. The New Deal for Communities regeneration programme (DCLG, 2010) for example, provided substantial evidence that *'in areas where people feel more of a part of their community there are better educational attainment outcomes'* (Taylor, 2008). Other networking and locality initiatives created by the Labour Government before 2010 were more directly concerned with the association between schools and communities. From 2007, every maintained school had a duty to promote community cohesion in a statutory response to an outburst of social unrest, not least in relatively deprived and socially segregated areas in the North of England. *The Children's Plan* (DCSF, 2007a) outlined the then government's 10-year strategy to make England the best place in the world for children and families. It noted that schools are *'well placed to become a focal point for the local community and to foster better relationships between diverse communities'* (ibid.: 73). Its aim then was that, by 2010, every primary and secondary school in England would be actively involved in designing and procuring, if not providing, a range of extended services for children and families (DCSF, 2007b). Two years later, the policy paper *Your child, your schools, our future: building a 21st century schools system* (DCSF, 2009b) maintained the Labour Government's emphasis on schools contributing to family well-being and community cohesion, referring to *'new forms of partnerships between schools and with other services'* (p 42) and the creation of services *'to support schools at the heart of their community'* (ibid.: 91 and 92). The government's suggestion was that schools could build links with their local communities in three ways which, we will show, reflected the work which had already been modelled by the PV leaders:

- through teaching, learning and the curriculum
- through promoting equity and excellence for all to succeed at the highest level
- through engagement and extended services that encourage positive interactions between different groups within their local community: *'opportunities for pupils, families and the wider community to take part in activities and receive services which build positive interaction and achievement for all groups'* (DCSF, 2007c: 7).

An unintended but apparently important consequence for the relationship between schools and their communities was the by-product of another policy. The policy was the encouragement for schools to employ classroom assistants, now usually called teaching assistants; the consequence was a new bond between schools and local neighbourhoods. In England, over the decade leading up to 2010, the full time equivalent (fte) number of teachers in publicly funded schools rose by 11 per cent to 448,000 (DfE, 2011c). In comparison, the number of fte teaching assistants increased by a remarkable 171 per cent from 79,000 to 214,000 while the fte of 'other support staff' more than doubled to 188,000. In 2000, almost three-quarters of the fte school workforce were teachers; by 2010, the total fte workforce in schools had increased by 43 per cent and barely half of the total were qualified to teach. In our experience, confirmed by PV leaders, the influx of comparatively low paid adults appears to have been sourced mainly from local communities, not least in areas of relative deprivation.

> *Teaching assistants often provide continuity between classes for both pupils and teachers and help to maintain the stability of relationships that pupils need… They often have a strong pastoral role and community links which are more informal than those of the teacher.*
> (Ofsted, 2002: 17)

Despite concerns about the variable impact of teaching assistants (Blatchford 2012) there is still potential for a beneficial connection between schools and communities when the former have become significant local employers. The stories these new staff tell about the school in the local supermarket queue might be more important for its local image than any league table or inspection report.

The Coalition Government rebranded the Department for Children Schools and Families as the Department for Education as soon as it took office in May 2010 – a decision which was widely interpreted as reflecting the incoming administration's doubts about schools' involvement in wider children's services, family or community matters. The Coalition has appeared to maintain the importance of the five outcomes for children signalled in its predecessor's Every Child Matters campaign (health, safety, enjoying and achieving, positively contributing and economic well-being) more in the breach than in the observance and without actively promoting service links between them. Secretary of State for Education, Michael Gove, described those five outcomes in a typical comment as '…*unimpeachable gospel [which] every teacher will want to do… I've got no problems with Every Child Matters as a list, but I do think it's important that we recognise that it should be policed in a hands-off way*' (Hansard, 2010).

The Coalition has also scrapped the ContactPoint child database which was unifying information about children across services, refocused

SureStart Children's Centres, removed the duty on Children's Trusts to produce an integrated local plan and removed the statutory requirement for schools to cooperate with Children's Trusts. If these changes reflect an emphasis which focuses schools on their core of teaching and learning, then arguably the Coalition's promotion of the 'Big Society' – in which outsourcing and a slimmer state seem to be key features – is consistent with schools choosing, but not being mandated, to engage with wider communities and, of course, vice versa: communities with schools. The Coalition's flagship policy for schools – the encouragement for all to take Academy status – also embraces a commitment to partnership and community activity:

> *Academies have to ensure that the school will be at the heart of its community, collaborating and sharing facilities and expertise with other schools and the wider community.*
>
> *We expect all high-performing schools applying for academy status to partner a weaker school. Collaboration and partnership are now embedded in the school system, and this is also the case for academies.*
> (DfE, 2011d)

Whether that too is to be *'policed in a hands-off way'* remains to be seen at the time of writing.

In summary, different governments take different, though ostensibly positive, approaches to the work of schools with their communities and the creation of public value, though they consistently demand improving educational performance. PV leaders consistently value their work with local people and believe it contributes to improving a range of outcomes for young people. They take whatever national capacity is available and flex it to that ambition.

Institutional capacity

PV leaders can and do work on institutional capacity with a more direct engagement than for national capacity. They want to influence governors who have the legal mandate for strategic oversight of the school and *'can also play an important role in establishing strong links with their local communities'* (Ofsted, 2010b: 52).

The importance and effectiveness of school governing bodies in the English education system is notably under researched. Handbooks describing the technicalities of their work abound and there are many subjective accounts of individual bodies. About a fifth of headteachers have described their governing body as very effective and a similar proportion described it as ineffective (PWC, 2007). Good governance is positively associated with higher pupil attainment (Ofsted, 2010b), though more significantly so in the primary phase than in the secondary (James *et al.*, 2010: 30). There is less evidence of objective description or analysis to show how governing bodies work or why they work well, or not (Earley and Creese, 2003). The quality of individual governing bodies appears to make some difference (Lord *et al.*, 2009), though that might be attributed to one or two governors rather than the governing body corporately (Earley, 2003; Earley *et al.*, 2002). The dynamic of cause and effect is not clear and a self-sustaining multiplier between pupil attainment, professional leadership and governance is a possible explanation (James *et al.*, 2010: Ch5). Given the tendency for governance to be reportedly weaker than leadership in more than a fifth of schools (Ofsted, 2010a), there is good reason to believe that the multiplier is working from the professional leadership towards the governors rather than vice versa. *'All the research into governing bodies agreed that the crucial factor in [their] effectiveness is the attitude of the head'* (Earley, 1998: 33). It is therefore no surprise to discover that in the 10 schools which participated in the enquiry the contribution of the governors was described by Ofsted as outstanding or good in nine cases and satisfactory in the tenth.

Although the creation of public value is by no means limited to work with disadvantaged communities, the schools in the public value enquiry tended to serve areas of (or with pockets of) relative poverty. That created additional challenges to governor recruitment and development when overall: *'... the research indicates that the majority of school governors are male, white and have professional or managerial backgrounds'* (Tomlinson, 2000: 30).

In the more challenging areas, this begs the question of where any institutional capacity, still less new capacity, will come from. While it would be wrong to second guess, in truth to stereotype, the skills, attitudes or empathy of individual governors or localities, there is a history of research showing that the composition of governing bodies in schools in poorer areas is less likely to be local and less likely to share characteristics with the student body (Streatfield and Jefferies, 1989; Keys and Fernandes, 1990).

> *In areas of socio-economic disadvantage, for instance, schools are under enormous pressure, both because their role in overcoming disadvantage is crucial and because the challenges they face are almost overwhelming. Yet it is in precisely such areas that the model of volunteer citizens supporting and challenging the work of professionals seems most problematic. Where are these volunteers to come from, given the pressures under which people in such areas find themselves?*
>
> (Dean *et al.*, 2007: 6)

The answer from the PV leaders has been, of course, that the people who constitute institutional capacity should be locally recruited and developed to become what might be categorised as associates rather than trustees, directors or activists.

- Trustees: watchdogs who trust the headteacher to run the school unless there are reasons to be concerned.
- Directors: a board which takes the strategic decisions, but leaves the executive action to the managing director (headteacher).
- Activists: who 'are the masters now', elected to run the school on behalf of all or possibly a faction of parents.
- Associates: who want to work alongside the professional staff, sharing ideas and expertise, working towards a collective interest rather than a consumer or managerial interest.

(Based on Knight, 1993)

Associates, substituted here instead of Knight's original use of 'partners', is a term we have used to describe people working in relationships based on trust and commitment rather than status and power (Mongon and Chapman, 2012). A governing body which is working in association with its professional staff *'socially aware, nurturing the school as a community in its own right, as a member of its neighbourhood community and as a unit in a wider professional community'* (ibid.: 23) is more likely, it seems to us, to be inclined to work in sincere partnership with the wider community and other agencies.

The relationship between headteachers and governors is of paramount importance in releasing the added value that newly recruited governors can provide and a key factor in governors feeling valued (Punter and Adams, undated). PV leaders nurture that relationship as best they can within the legal framework for governance in English schools. We turn now to look at how they build personal, associate and contextual capacity and to do so we need to outline a five task framework.

The five task framework

With the help of the PV leaders, we have identified five key tasks which created new capacity around their work.

1. Developing internal capacity (core teaching and learning).
2. Drawing on and enhancing community capacity.
3. Reaching out to generate community capacity.
4. Investing outwards to create community capital.
5. Speculating to sponsor community capital.

These tasks are neither hierarchical nor sequential: the balance of activity across the tasks will vary from school to school and over time; often they will overlap and interlink. All the PV schools began with a focus on the first task, teaching and learning, and then moved on from there in whatever sequence and with whatever emphasis suited their context. Context here is so critical that a politician might be tempted to say *'It's the context, stupid!'* or even *'context, context, context'* – we will resist that. Our use of the five tasks and the model we have designed to illustrate their connectivity (Figure 5.2, p80) are therefore not prescriptive, even though they are proving to be valuable aides to enquiry, reflection and action.

We will briefly outline each of the five tasks before considering specific examples and how each type of task contributes to the development of new capacity in the personal, associate or contextual dimensions. The public value enquiry was essentially an enquiry into what already existed, so the specific examples were not generated by it. They are therefore summarised in the past tense and attributed to the school which reported them during the enquiry.

> **Task 1: Developing internal capacity: to improve the core activity, teaching and learning, measured by standard educational attainments and prescribed accountability.**

The first of the five tasks is to lead and to manage the school's core capacity in order to deliver effective teaching and learning so that standards of attainment improve or remain high. All the PV leaders told us that securing a baseline of good standards is essential to winning space for innovation in other aspects of the school's work. We propose elsewhere that secure, conventional success is rarely the impetus for radical work but, in relatively conventional settings, it can quickly become the touchstone by which outside agencies judge innovation. In any case, the PV leaders see the learning of children and young people as the school's core compact with families and local communities, without which anything else they attempt is undermined. Education settings that let basic standards slip, they reported, risk losing the legitimacy and support from key stakeholders, not least the local community, which is needed to undertake any wider community-based work.

> *You need to get that short-term fix on attainment but you need to make sure that the long-term vision is there otherwise the short-term will just fall flat. You need to recognise that you're going to hit a plateau unless you invest time, money and resources into developing social capital and public value.*
> Roger Whittall, Headteacher, The Westwood Secondary School

The provision of good teaching and learning was a constant work in progress for the PV schools: regular, incremental improvements had been offset by occasional setbacks not least for some of the schools which serve very disadvantaged communities. Two schools associated with the enquiry have skirted the edge of disappointing Ofsted judgements and then recovered. The PV leaders returned regularly to the question of whether any cost in time or money on any activity they chose to sponsor outside the classroom – still more so outside the school – would add to the outcomes for which they are directly held accountable – end of Key Stage assessments. At the very least they needed to be confident that the activities would not diminish those outcomes. They are risk takers but they are not rash. At times when these leaders had their attention and personal effort drawn beyond the emphasis on teaching and learning, they needed to be confident that someone in their leadership team had the capacity and capability to take good care of that core work.

In this context, personalised learning becomes an increasingly vital link between members of the school community and members of the neighbourhood community (some of whom will be in both). Personalised learning based on a wider curriculum, alternative forms of assessment and more collaborative, exploratory and real-world learning is more likely to make it possible for the community to engage with its school and to make a school more relevant to its community. Schools which are heavily regulated professional enclaves offer little, if any, space for external, non-teacher involvement in their work. Student voice, in particular, is on a continuum with community voice, and leaders who are open to one appear more likely to engage with both to good effect.

The medium is also the message for PV leaders and that means their colleagues' development and their own development are also strong features of their approach. (It is to some degree an explanation for their willingness to engage in the public value enquiry.) Without compromising their authority or sense of purpose, the PV leaders appeared to be searching for the space where both adults and young people can exercise initiative spontaneously and collaboratively and so, in learning at least, the demarcation between leaders and followers does not need to be well defined. MacBeath uses 'symbiosis' to describe these reciprocal relationships in which there is an implicit give and take and a level of mutual respect: *'While delegation is expressed in "giving" responsibility to others or allowing responsibility by structural default, symbiosis has a more organic quality'* (MacBeath, 2008: 53).

Task 1: Developing internal capacity to improve teaching and learning reflected the PV schools' commitment to pupils' attainment being as good as possible. The leaders in those schools did the things most school leaders recognise. They had adapted their approach to suit their context and they placed great importance on quality. The following are some examples of their core teaching and learning response to local circumstances.

At **Clifton Green Primary School** the most successful from the range of activities to improve reading skills across whole year groups proved to be those in which children had received help from their parents. In addition, the school had identified work to address the needs of families arriving from overseas as a priority area for both the school and the local community. It decided therefore to use personalised learning resources to offer one-to-one tuition by qualified teachers to a small group of children for whom English was an additional language. The approach proved so successful that it was extended to redress other inequalities and the school allocated additional resources to tutor similarly a group of socially disadvantaged pupils who had not made the progress it would have liked.

Coleshill Heath Primary School developed physical education and sport as a way of engaging pupils, staff, parents and the whole community, and as a driver to raise attainment through high quality curricular and extra-curricular provision. Over about five years, PE curricular time increased threefold from 60 minutes a week to a minimum of 180 minutes. Success in sport is encouraging achievement on a much wider scale and is raising pupils' confidence in other areas of their learning.

George Green's Secondary School introduced a community-based course called Learn2Learn. The course was designed and taught by the director of extended services for a group of Year 7 students who were identified as experiencing real difficulties with learning and who were likely, without intervention, to become disengaged from school. The course, running one day a week, had been tailor-made for the group, using the school's knowledge of the local community and building on its connection with local networks.

St Thomas's Centre Pupil Referral Unit used fishing as a motivating activity for its students, as a way to provide aspects of its science, geography and craft, design and technology programmes, and as a potential route to a GNVQ qualification. The project, which started with a pupil-led feasibility study, provided a framework for developing a range of skills through activities, including applying for grant funding, planning exercises, developing environmental awareness and report writing.

> **Task 2: Drawing on and enhancing capacity from within the community, supplementing and complementing resources which have been formally delegated or allocated to the school.**

The second task is to complement the core capacity of the school by drawing on and enhancing capacity from within the community. This pre-existing capacity becomes new capacity by virtue of its deployment in new circumstances, inside rather than outside the school. It is capacity the school can mobilise – people, skills, facilities, technology – but which it does not own or control. This (like other tasks in this list) aims to provide a richer and more relevant learning experience for young people. The wider the range of sources from which this capacity can be drawn then the richer the range of options to mix internal and external capacity in new forms. The PV leaders insisted that this is not a matter of whether the community has capacity – they would argue every community does – it is a matter of judging where to drill the wells and how to tap them.

With both this task and the following one, the PV leaders did not regard the work that was creating public value as additional to their basic work. They did not ask whether they should do 'core *or* extended' or even whether they should do 'core *plus* extended'. For them the two are inextricably linked and the core can only work well *with* the extended – and vice versa. For these leaders it is not a question of whether they should engage with the world beyond the school walls: they know it is swept through the school door every morning on a tide of pupils with all its undercurrents of health, well-being, housing, happiness, economic security, family dynamics, employment, wealth and children's services connections.

> **Task 2: Drawing on and enhancing community capacity – requires engagement with the people, skills, facilities and technology around educational settings that can be used, on or off site, to directly enrich the learning experience of children and young people and contribute directly to meeting the targets for social or academic attainment. The following are illustrations of how the PV leaders did that.**

Brixham Community College drew deeply on the local West Country history of coastal industry and creativity. Its 'Red Sails in the Sunset' project was run by a group of local volunteers ambitious to keep the tradition of sailing boats alive within the area. Students produced a DVD and marketing materials on sailing boats and their contribution to the local economy, people's livelihoods and local traditions. As a spin-off from that activity, the Red Sails in the Sunset group facilitated a programme aimed at engaging the most disaffected young people in Year 10. The young people took part in a vocational programme with a practical application to the fishing industry, run by volunteers.

When **Clifton Green Primary School** wanted to know more about what it could do to help children and families from overseas settle into school, it turned to its parent governors to provide new capacity. The parent governors volunteered to approach a number of families to get their first-hand accounts of what it was like to be a new resident in that community and the initial needs and anxieties they had. As a result, the governing body's diversity group asked the parent governors to become buddies to new parents to help their induction to school. The initiative has helped the school know precisely how to target resources to improve provision for newly arriving children. The children's centre partnership board, which includes parents, governors, health service providers, the centre manager and school leaders is also a vital broker between the education setting and its partners. The partnership board sponsors community partnership events to explore community issues, a parents' self-help group and a local leadership group comprising all the managers of staff located on the site.

Coleshill Heath Primary School used its approach to PE and Sport as one way to develop the skills of an increasing number of local employees The school invested in training for dinner supervisors so that they could develop and provide quality sports activities alongside identified pupil leaders who control the play resources. One former pupil progressed from being a support assistant to becoming a PE specialist and the school's extended schools sports co-ordinator. When other local people wanted to work with the children at Coleshill Heath and to learn new skills to enhance their employability, the school set about enabling them to acquire the necessary qualifications. The invitation to Solihull Further Education (FE) College to run classes in childcare became part of the FE college's community offer in an eventually thriving on-site adult education base with ICT facilities.

Delaware Community Primary School tapped into local business expertise as part of a school-wide business project in which every class designed, created and sold its own products. A local potter, a catering manager from the local community college and a manager from a national pasty firm were invited to share their management skills with children across all age groups. The professional business input helped pupils develop a better understanding of value for money and profit and loss scenarios. Each class developed their own product of choice including calendars, recipe books and greetings cards. They then held a community business fair and sold the goods they had produced to raise more than £1,000 for FARM-Africa (see www.farmafrica.org.uk). The benefits spun off beyond the children's own learning into stronger links between the school and the business community.

At **George Green's Secondary School**, the community team comprised support workers supervised by the youth and community manager. Some of the team worked within local organisations and were not directly employed by the school but all were representative of the local community and lived or worked on the Isle of Dogs. The team was funded via the school's youth service contract. Part of their work was to create activities for Year 7 students in unstructured time, typically at lunchtime. The playground was an effective training ground for youth workers who were accustomed to working in a very different setting and the work is having a positive effect on relationships, community cohesion and individual student achievement.

St Thomas's Centre Pupil Referral Unit found many parents were not accessing local GP, dentist and optician services for their children for a variety of reasons, including time constraints, inability to register and indifference, and pupils didn't know how to access facilities on their own. The headteacher contacted the health authority and secured a dedicated school nurse who provides weekly drop-in sessions at the school where pupils can access information and confidential advice. The deputy head used her pupil knowledge to encourage those in need of services to attend. The sessions were always busy, and successes included several examples of securing health interventions for pupils who would not otherwise have been treated.

Task 3: Reaching out to generate community capacity, developing the ability of immediate social networks and families to help enhance performance, pupil attendance and attitude. This external investment generates new capacity with direct pay backs.

The third task is to invest some of the capacity at the school's disposal in work with local families, parents and social networks, where there is a case that this community outreach and support work could pay dividends for the school's core work. A clear example of this is the trend to employ parental support workers to work with parents at home or in other places outside the school, in the hope that this will improve their capacity and motivation to support their children's approach to learning. In many places, this investment has been made easier by working collaboratively with other providers of children's services from the public or other sectors. PV leaders gather the resources for this work from a variety of sources including the basic school budget, grants and bids, wider community initiatives, charges made to service users and the support of other agencies and providers.

> We had been steadily improving attendance and attainment to the level where we were judged to be outstanding. We had celebrated our achievements with parents and the community, a real partnership effort. A local survey then revealed just how limited the ambitions of our successful pupils were – low paid work and teenage pregnancies. It struck us that after all of our work on raising attainment, our children and community had not understood what this could mean for their life chances and future options.
>
> Sheila Audsley, Headteacher, Clifton Green Primary School

> **Task 3: Reaching out to generate community capacity – requires the school to deploy time or money in support of an activity which may not be directly related to classroom teaching and learning but is a purposeful investment that can reasonably be expected to improve outcomes in school and, by doing so, across the community. The following are illustrations of how the PV leaders did that.**

Castle Children's Centre seconded two staff to map the services and professional and voluntary groups working in the centre's reach. The complex exercise allowed the centre to collaborate with agencies that had similar aims and objectives to its own, as well as other agencies that were keen to network. The centre's aim was to engage more directly with the disadvantaged local community which is predominantly black and minority ethnic. The centre used bilingual staff or volunteers to run taster sessions – demonstrations of the centre's work – in local community centres. This design built on the centre's successful traveller project which had introduced a traveller liaison officer and used agencies and connections trusted by both the providers and the traveller community to work actively, outside the centre, to nurture the families' interest in the centre. The result had been an increase in traveller registrations not only at the centre but also at the local primary school.

Clifton Green Primary School ran a careers fair for the whole community to raise aspiration and attainment. Parents, grandparents, children and students from York University were involved in chatting about jobs and university.

Coleshill Heath Primary School had an open-door policy so that parents, carers and children could come into school without an appointment and be seen by a designated member of staff at any time to discuss school or home issues. The school also employed a Senior Child and Family Support Worker. The aim was to break down barriers to learning and to raise trust levels. In support of that, the school offered an in-depth therapeutic course, 'Mellow Parenting', of 15 weeks, reflecting on the effects of 'the way we were parented' and the impact that has had on the way we parent our children. It also offered the 'Solihull Approach': a course looking at behaviour and ways of understanding behaviour, and 'Solution Focused Brief Therapy' which focused on solutions rather than problems.

Delaware Community Primary School employed and line managed a parent support adviser (PSA) funded by an extended services network of 11 schools. Delaware's ambition was to help the wider community and the cluster of schools – as well as itself – by meeting the cash and time costs of hosting the PSA. The PSA's role was to offer direct support to families in whatever way possible, daytime or evening, formal or informal. The PSA provided a range of open-house sessions at the school, including a post-natal group and toddler group. Delaware also offered a range of activities, mostly self-funded, to promote learning across the wider community outside school hours. Themes included yoga, a rock school and music tuition, unicycle hockey, cookery for teenagers and genealogy. Evening adult education classes also nurtured new relationships between the school and community.

Garforth Community College – in alliance with four primary schools, the local further education college, the primary care trust and the Learning and Skills Council Schools – created a trust to provide the legal vehicle within which to invest time and money for a community focused collaborative. Each of the school governing bodies remained focused on teaching and learning while the trust provided a vehicle for shared activity across a range of children's services. The trust also provided the hub to share planning, facilities and provision to guarantee the core extended services offer to families across the locality. The trust can also sponsor local enterprise, including its own retail sites, to improve the personalised curriculum offer to young people.

George Green's Secondary School, like many schools in the public value enquiry, was a significant local employer: fewer than half of its 200-plus staff were teachers. The school's extended services included management of the area youth service (won on competitive tender), health advice, family therapy, school home support, safer school partnership (a police officer), social work, attendance welfare, learning mentors, young carers support, volunteers, Connexions and other employment advice.

In another part of London's East End, **Swanlea Business and Enterprise College** had used its strong community links to create activities inside and outside the core curriculum, including, for example, being the launch venue for National Social Enterprise Day, a 'Female Asian Entrepreneur' event and the 'Ambassadors Programme' (female entrepreneurs visiting the school). Students' attendance at the school was a priority shared with the East London Mosque – a shared concern for a small number of students, sometimes in families at the margins of social, cultural and educational engagement. The School designed a service level agreement with the Mosque for work with these families which became a model for a service offered to other schools

Westwood Secondary School abandoned the conventional parents' association when it became too exclusive and over focused on social activities with benefits for only a few adults. A community working party, representing the university, community police, neighbourhood management, project champions, community engagement officers and people from the Canley regeneration project, began meeting in the school once every half term. As a team they looked at creating opportunities for the students not only to become more involved in the community but also to develop cohesion between the various partners. The 12 areas identified for Community Action were translated into active projects.

Task 4: Investing outwards to create social capital and capacity in the community. This generates paybacks for the school but the effect is less direct and longer term

The fourth task is to invest some of the school's capacity in helping to build wider social capital and to improve cohesion – engaging with people beyond the parents and families connected to the educational setting. This includes, for example, helping to run adult learning classes or providing their facilities as a venue for local voluntary groups. The pay-off from this investment is likely to be longer term and less direct. Schools and centres cannot on their own change communities or resolve deep and underlying social and economic inequalities. But they can play a role, with other agencies, in helping to build up social capital in areas where it is in decline.

> First and foremost you are an educator. To educate you have to remove as many barriers to learning as is required for the pupils in your care so that they can access education. It is their human right. You cannot remove barriers on your own. Engage all the help and expertise from the whole of the community to support the whole of the child.
>
> Margaret Nowell, Headteacher, St Thomas's Centre Pupil Referral Unit

PV schools play a key role in creating networks across the school, neighbourhood and service provider communities. They provide what has been described as *'a powerful way of engaging the community and creating greater community cohesion… a conduit for provision and an important way of connecting schools, families and communities together….an influential infrastructure for securing improved wellbeing and creating greater community cohesion'* (Statham *et al.*, 2010).

The PV leaders' approach to Tasks 3, 4 and 5 were usually based on horizon scanning and testing of ideas with the local community and its representatives. Almost every form of imaginable conversation, encounter, meeting, event, activity, questionnaire and poll had been used at some time by one or other of the PV leaders to acquire local insight. They had then designed and tailored, usually in another collaborative exercise, a specifically local approach to the issues which emerged. The activities they then supported showed respect and sensitivity for their context without slipping into the professional trap of being patronising or condescending. Of a similar group of school leaders, it has been written that:

> *They tend to talk about the strengths of the local community rather than its weaknesses, they see the locality as an opportunity rather than a problem, they approach the area as a resource rather than an obstacle. They have a clear, all round view of their position in local educational networks. They understand the political environments in which they operate, locally and nationally.*
>
> (Mongon and Chapman, 2008).

Task 4: Investing outwards to create community capital – generates activities which will have an indirect impact on educational attainment but possibly some direct impact on other outcomes for young people by nurturing the positive aspects of family and neighbourhood life which correlate with improved attainment and other outcomes. The following are illustrations of how the PV leaders did that.

The community being served by **Castle Children's Centre** had been badly affected by debt, not a matter with which schools might normally feel they could help. However, the problem was affecting the motivation and well-being of families – and therefore children – so badly that the centre established a credit union on the school site. Originally directed at adults, it eventually offered accounts to children, encouraging them to develop good financial habits. The centre also ran sessions and promoted information on how to manage a family budget while a Citizens' Advice Bureau representative attended the centre weekly to advise on benefit claims, tax credits, the Child Trust Fund, etc.

Coleshill Heath Primary School organised a small fleet of extended services community vehicles including minibuses, a small family vehicle and a high roofed van, known locally as the 'smiley van'. The fleet was used to help ensure regular attendance at school by pupils who might not otherwise attend and to help children, particularly those from families in greatest need, attend residential trips. The vehicles had also been used to transport furniture for a young parent making a first move to independent accommodation and by support workers from other services who needed to transport pushchairs and wheelchairs to family appointments. On a different project, the school's leaders worked with play development workers from other services on the development of a new adventure playground in Solihull, eventually to be managed by a parent and community group.

Delaware Community Primary School led the establishment of an on-site learning centre and community resource for the village and the rural locality it serves. Called the Delaware Community Learning Centre, it houses a children's centre and a pre-school and adult learning complex. The centre hosts ante-natal and post-natal checks, health visitor and baby weigh-in clinics, social groups and advice services, as well as a centre for jobseekers and training for parents to help them with parenting skills. It also hosts a community café, public access computers, WiFi and three rooms available for hire for events, club meetings and so on. It offers round-the-clock facilities where local people of any age can sponsor or participate in a range of activities offering more or less formal learning opportunities. To achieve this, the school leadership drew an originally diffident community into a close partnership, establishing a not-for-profit company to house the activity and inviting parents to take leading roles. The Learning Centre has been developed in close consultation with the community and included a community learning centre with a children's centre. A representative committee was formed to oversee the management of the centre, but aligning the expectations of the children's centre funding, family services and a pre-school provider with the very wide range of community interest groups made substantial demands on school leaders who had to arbitrate the emotional and legal ownership of space.

Westwood Secondary School had been an active member of the local Canley Stakeholders' Forum and Canley Community Forum, which connects the schools with a wide range of local organisations leading or supporting key community events as part of the Canley Regeneration Project. Groups of students from Westwood trained to be community ambassadors, which gave them insight into community cohesion and cultural diversity issues.

Garforth Community College's trust-owned uniform and equipment shop also served as an ICT training hub for the community's learning platform. The community used the platform to access information, for example about council or health services. By undergoing training in its effective use, parents developed their own IT and internet skills and were consequently better able to support their own learning and that of their children.

Task 5: Speculating to nurture community capital – making resources available for community activities and new community capacity. With no obvious direct or indirect payback, this is an act of well-informed faith from which most of the value and new capacity escapes into the community.

The fifth task is to make resources available as a platform for community activities that will generate community benefits with little, if any, direct payback to the school. This task might include, for example, providing a base for community meetings, self-help classes, organic food schemes and cultural events. This grows out of a sense of social responsibility and a desire, even if not expressed in these terms, to create the greatest possible public value from public assets. It is, to all intents and purposes, impossible to pin down the value this approach creates; most of that spins out into the community rather than being internalised back in the school. The act of faith is that reciprocity will come from building a sense of common interest around the school and a willingness to support its core and community work.

> **Task 5: Speculating to sponsor community capital** – making resources available with no obvious direct payback depends on schools' commitments to community and the opportunities they create altruistically for local people. Their aim is to enhance community well-being and build community cohesion. They are unlikely to impact directly on attainment, but they do build social capital and the school's standing in the community. The following are illustrations of how the PV leaders did that.
>
> **Coleshill Heath Primary School** decided to offer its facilities for community use after research with the West Midlands police revealed an increase in antisocial behaviour during INSET days. Pupils now have the opportunity to take part in street dance, basketball and football sessions delivered by local coaches and clubs.
>
> Café Vert was the trading name of the eating and lifestyle outlet within **George Green's Secondary School.** The not-for-profit social enterprise scheme provided a vocational training café for pupils and their families, and the young people involved also offer a catering service to local businesses. The Café, designed by young people in collaboration with an architect, was a venue for a range of in-school, special education needs and disabilities (SEND), youth service, community and regional activities.
>
> At the **Westwood Secondary School** a member of the leadership team had responsibility for community development and cohesion in order to ensure that the theme is embedded in the school's curricular and extra-curricular planning. The school had been working with a range of external services to promote community cohesion in response to increasingly racist violence in the local community. It had provided facilities to create a school-based youth service and, in an illustration of how the five tasks often overlap, community police officers who had a permanent office on site (Task 5) led on whole-school events and extra-curricular activities (Task 3).

Figure 5.2 illustrates the complex way in which the five tasks interact with one another, more or less directly connected to the core of teaching and learning.

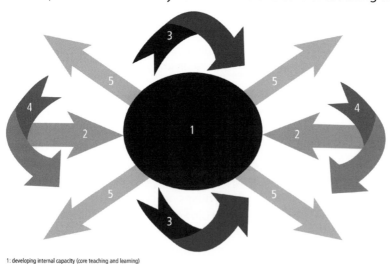

1: developing internal capacity (core teaching and learning)
2: drawing on and enhancing community capacity
3: reaching out to generate community capacity
4: investing outwards to create community capital
5: speculating to sponsor community capital

Figure 5.2: A five-task framework

New capacity: personal, associate and contextual elements

The new capacity generated by the five tasks we have described can be categorised as predominantly personal, associate or contextual capacity. Some will translate into the formal governance arrangements of the school – institutional capacity – but, as we wrote earlier, even that will manifest itself as associate capacity. National capacity is hardly influenced by local tasks and, if this does happen, it is never speedy. To a very large degree, the creation of institutional and national capacity is stuck firmly in the top left hand quadrant of the education innovation grid which we introduced in Chapter 2 (Table 2.1). They mainly contribute to IMPROVEMENT by technical innovation in formal learning. They contribute little to disruptive innovation or to informal settings and so have little impact on SUPPLEMENTING and even less on REINVENTING or TRANSFORMING educational activity.

The personal capacity of effective PV leaders and others who contribute in every quadrant of the education innovation grid owes, by definition, a great deal to the leaders' own commitment and energy and also to their experience and learning. Its basic form often, though not always, owes a great deal to their origins (Mongon and Chapman, 2008) and, as we proposed in the previous chapter, to their self-confidence and conscientiousness. PV leaders use their sense of ambitious curiosity to create new capacity for themselves. Ambitious curiosity is the compelling need to understand what works so that practice can be improved. That compulsion also infuses their expectations of the adults around them and translates into an enthusiasm for personal and communal learning that adults can share with one another and with their students. The PV leaders' involvement in the National College enquiry which has informed our writing is evidence of their willingness to find the time for reflecting on their work, sharing it with others and creating new insights.

A point which needs to be made about new personal capacity, and which also leaks into associate and contextual capacity, is that in order to promote public value all three require the people involved to feel comfortable with leadership which is more associative – a term used to indicate a basis of trust and mutual respect (Mongon and Chapman, 2012) – than managerial – based on command and control. This is partly a personal and partly a communal disposition with which people need to feel comfortable, whether they are in an apparently powerful or less powerful role and whenever they move from one to the other.

In particular and as we have already noted, the further the roles adopted by school leaders move from the core of teaching and learning on a single school site, the more adaptive, by which we mean outside traditional custom and practice, both the leadership and governance arrangements need to be. This comes into sharp focus when education professionals are working with 'lay' members of the community or with professionals from other disciplines whose values and ambitions will probably not coincide exactly with the school's culture and targets. The PV leaders told us that any leader striving to employ principles of equity, fairness and empowerment will inevitably build relationships on that basis not only with staff and pupils but with governors, families, community representatives and other service providers. Where this distributive approach does not apply, school leaders will become overworked and find themselves at 'saturation point' (Wilkin et al., 2007).

The general shift from management to leadership across the five tasks is illustrated in Figure 5.3. This shows that as the leading actors move from tasks which are core to the school towards tasks which are increasingly community based, there is a related and general trend for the element of managerialism to reduce and the element of association to increase.

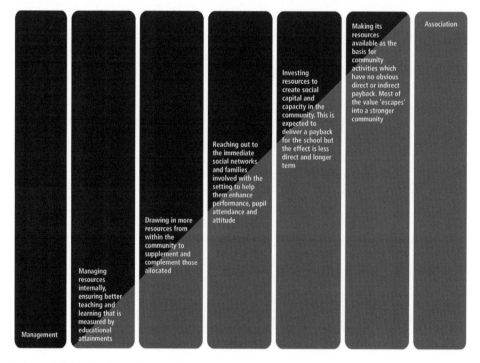

Making its resources available as the basis for community activities which have no obvious direct or indirect payback. Most of the value 'escapes' into a stronger community

Association

Investing resources to create social capital and capacity in the community. This is expected to deliver a payback for the school but the effect is less direct and longer term

Reaching out to the immediate social networks and families involved with the setting to help them enhance performance, pupil attendance and attitude

Drawing in more resources from within the community to supplement and complement those allocated

Managing resources internally, ensuring better teaching and learning that is measured by educational attainments

Management

Figure 5.3: Leadership – from management to association

Associate capacity is derived from the synergy of an educational community working in harmony or, since perfection is as good an idea – and about as realistic – as a perpetual-motion machine, working with minimum friction. It is the key, though not the only driver for Tasks 1 and 2 – the core of teaching and learning alongside the drawing in of community capacity. It is generally focused on the IMPROVEMENT and REINVENTION quadrants of the innovation grid (Table 2.1) but is capable of harbouring activity which SUPPLEMENTS or even TRANSFORMS a school's work. The social capital of teachers (akin to what we are calling association) has been reported as a significant predictor of student achievement gains that are above and beyond teacher experience or ability in the classroom – and its effect was powerful (Leana, 2011).

New associate capacity is created by adults who share their leadership's sense of curiosity about what works. We referred earlier to Watkin *et al.*'s distinction between a performance orientation and a learning orientation (2007). The latter focused on a belief in self-motivated learning leading to improvement, a preference for challenge and deep personal satisfaction with success in the face of adversity. Watkins's thesis is that the personalised and internalised strategies of a learning orientation have a deeper and more enduring effect on performance than institutionalised and externalised strategies motivated by compliance. That thesis is true for adults and young people alike. The research shows that promoting and participating in teacher learning and development has twice the positive impact of any other leadership strategy (Robinson *et al.*, 2009: 38). The PV schools had a critical mass of adults who shared that view and who were eager not only to improve their own classroom craft but also to experiment with the ways in which closer community engagement could enhance a wider range of outcomes for their pupils.

The creation of new contextual capacity is a profound challenge to the cliché of helplessness and inadequacy which is associated with many of the neighbourhoods served by the PV schools and similar areas. That is a cliché because, of course, it does have some basis in reality but it is also a caricature because it unfairly distorts reality. Writing about life on such estates Lynsey Hanley, author of *Estates, an Intimate History* (Hanley, 2007) has commented:

> If you live and are educated in such an area, you may as well live in a penal colony for all that it connects you with a world in which good-quality work, self-confidence and cultural capital – that quality through which the middle classes perpetuate social and economic dominance – are a given.
>
> (Hanley, 2011)

Contextual capacity is created by 'collaborative advantage' which is, in effect, the reduction in duplication, the increases in efficiency, the additional effort and above all the generation of radical ideas which can be created by turning the differences between organisations or groups into synergy and new capacity. New contextual capacity can drive technical or disruptive innovation across three-quarters of the innovation grid (Table 2.1) by SUPPLEMENTING, REINVENTING or TRANSFORMING formal or informal educational arrangements. It is the key driver, though again not the only one, for Tasks 3, 4 and 5 – reaching out, investing and speculating. It is a route to augmenting resources, sharing risk, improving efficiency and coordinating activity between services, families and communities (Huxham and Vangen, 2005). It depends on schools and communities which do not simply expect the one to contribute to the other, but are constantly looking out for opportunities to contribute to one another because they recognise their interdependence.

> *What sense does it make to try to reform urban schools while the communities around them stagnate or collapse? Conversely, can community-building and development efforts succeed in revitalizing inner-city neighborhoods if the public schools within them continue to fail their students? The fates of urban schools and communities are linked, yet school reformers and community builders typically act as if they are not.*
>
> (Warren, 2005: 133)

Contextual capacity therefore pays a double dividend: to the school in meeting core targets around attendance, attitude and attainment as well as to families and networks through, for example, enhancing family learning, economic capacity and social cohesion. This is an international phenomenon: in the United States, community organising has created an opportunity for school-level improvement

> *by building support and pressure for school restructuring, reduced overcrowding, new teaching expertise, new curriculum mandates, and additional supports for parent and community engagement [leading to]… Improved student outcomes in the form of higher student attendance, improved test scores, increased graduation rates, and higher college-going aspirations.*
>
> (Mediratta et al., 2008: 6 and 7)

Creating contextual capacity is not necessarily innovative in its own right. Schools, we acknowledged in earlier chapters, have always been a significant resource for their communities although *'The enterprise, vision and energy that has gone into these developments, often in schools in difficult circumstances, has perhaps not been fully appreciated'* (Wilkin et al., 2003: 116). Again, it is the deployment of the school-sponsored contextual capacity which determines the extent to which it is new or adaptive. Most school leaders will admit to being concerned about the balance they need to find between the priorities of teaching and learning on the one hand and their school's contribution to students' well-being, partnerships and community regeneration on the other. New contextual capacity depends on schools which are not passive about the potential of a wider neighbourhood community or even about the wider provider community. The PV schools use the activities across Tasks 3, 4 and 5 – reaching out, investing and speculating in local development – to create the bonding and bridging capital from which they believe their core work benefits. As one school leader outside the public value group told us during another enquiry:

> Working with parents and the community, is how you create the right atmosphere. It's not just the encouragement parents will then give their own children, it's the contribution different adults make, in different kinds of ways, to our curriculum offer.
>
> (Mongon, 2010: 3)

With that summarising quote on new capacity we move on to *new measures of value.*

Chapter 6

Measuring for value

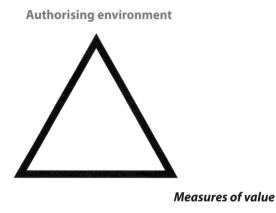

Authorising environment

New capacity   *Measures of value*

Figure 6.1: Measures of value in the 'public innovation triangle'.

Source: Based on Moore (1995). Used by permission.

In the previous two chapters, we reflected on the importance of authorising environments and new capacity for schools whose innovative work might increase the public value around them. The PV schools provided examples from their work to illustrate those two themes. We turn now to measures of value and the effect they have on practice, in particular innovative practice. Again, the PV schools are a key source for the work which informs our analysis.

> *How do you count the number of young people that you've 'saved' as a result of local knowledge and close partnership with social services? How do you count the number of young people who haven't been out in the streets stabbing each other because you've provided other things for them to do?*
> Stella Bailey, Director for Extended Services, George Green's Secondary School

There is widespread international recognition that evaluation and assessment frameworks are crucial to building stronger and fairer school systems. There is a similar consensus around the importance of ensuring that those frameworks do not become ends in themselves but are used as one of the means for achieving improved student outcomes (OECD, 2011a). The alternative is dire: inappropriate tools for evaluation and assessment will always inhibit and diminish outcomes. In Chapter 2 we proposed that measurement is first of all the ignition key for starting to understand the limitations of current, standard approaches and then an accelerator for demonstrating the value created by new approaches. Authorising environments crumble and new capacity evaporates unless there is valid evidence of progress in innovative practice. Innovation might well begin – and begin well – with intuition propelled by frustration and a belief that better solutions are possible – as they did when Dave Dunkley the Head at Coleshill Heath recruited a band of angry but eager parents from an area of high unemployment to help him turn the school around. Working as unpaid volunteers, the parents provided childcare, learning support as well as before- and after-school activities: training and then wages eventually followed. But, innovators usually need to operate and move to scale in established and perhaps even moribund systems. In those difficult circumstances, the costs and benefits of innovation need to be demonstrable to be sustained; individual passion and good intentions do help but, on their own, they do not change systems. Dave Dunkley did that by securing the quality of the innovation and public value in Coleshill Heath and used evidence from that to convince a network of neighbouring primary schools.

Dave Dunkley's activism and that of the other PV leaders is the operational confirmation of John Benington's assertion that authorisation to create public value *'has to be won and constantly replenished from a wide variety of different stakeholders, from different levels of government, and from different parts of the public, private, voluntary, and informal community sectors'* (Benington, 2009: 246). In effect, Benington argues, a public has to be created for public value to thrive. His proposition is that this requires development along three dimensions, key features of which can be summarised as follows:

- Political development to legitimate certain kinds of cultural values and activity (and de-legitimate others).
- Economic development to promote equity in the availability of resources and to stimulate disciplined innovation
- Social and community development to promote access for all through community development and active engagement in public and political life across a wide range of community organisations; orchestrating a wide group of partners and stakeholders in the public, private, voluntary, and informal community sector.

(Derived from Benington op. cit.: 247)

The PV leaders use that range of political, economic, social and community levers to create authorisation for the wider range of measures, still including attainment, against which they believe their work should be measured. They also argue that these processes, along with sustainable development, are inextricably intertwined not only with their core commitment to teaching, learning and attainment but also with the wider range of outcomes from their work for which they are prepared to be accountable. In fact, as became apparent, to some extent process and outcome become almost indistinguishable.

Using our five stage typology including personal, associate and contextual authorisation, it is axiomatic that the other two, institutional and national, will create measures of value with intrinsic *force majeure*. Institutional measures, applied in English schools by the governing body, will necessarily include those required by law even if some other wider outcomes creep in by local agreement. The measures required by national legislation seem to be almost inevitably and universally standardised, numeric and easy-to-measure performance indicators across a limited number of attainment outputs for young people. Against that background of powerfully authorised measures of value, the intrinsically personal and often moral or ethical measures which PV school leaders and their colleagues appear to apply struggle for airspace.

The associate measures of value – those around which the school community can rally – often invoke a sense of 'job well done'. This seems to be true for adults and students alike in the PV schools. Targets are not set and goals are not achieved in order to satisfy an external accountability (though it would be daft to suggest that is not lodged somewhere in the communal mind) but to satisfy an internal hunger for self-esteem. Contextual measures of value, those shared by provider and neighbourhood communities, are also partly composed of the institutional measures imposed by national policy and institutional authorisation on each of the partners. But other measures of value do emerge – some of those are what we will later describe as process outcomes, the creation of new relationships, cultures and modus operandi; others involve a social or emotional dimension which would be difficult to track even in a single organisation, even more so in a collaboration.

There are profound technical, political, professional, organisational and structural impediments to invoking new measures of value. In Chapter 2 we summarised those into six key challenges:

- **The measurement of inputs**: officially, national education inputs have three components: labour (for example teaching staff), goods and services (for example learning materials and electricity) and capital services (for example the provision of a vehicle or building in a given period). The total cost of those three inputs was estimated at £71 billion for the United Kingdom in 2009 (Baird *et al.*, 2010: 16). At school levels we can measure the inputs from teacher to pupil ratios, days or hours the school is open, materials used in classrooms. None of those official measures includes the direct or indirect contributions which are the result of parental commitment, peer influence, community culture and other unpaid 'inputs'. Given that estimates of the value of unpaid work range from about a third to three-quarters of GDP in the UK (OECD, 2011b: Fig 1.13) it would be fair to assume that the replacement or opportunity costs of these factors in education are at least hypothetically massive. Unfortunately, inputs of that sort are elusively difficult to measure despite being *'key channels for educational effects'* (Feinstein *et al.*, 2004). They are also difficult to categorise when we consider that some of that informal or unofficial input is arguably also an output of school effects, a consequence of schools creating public value. The result is that they remain under reported and underrated.

- **The measurement of outputs**: there are two dimensions to educational outputs: quantitative (in effect the number of students) and qualitative (in effect test results). In schools, we do not usually treat admissions as a measure of value except, occasionally, for a small number in a spiral of decline. For school quality, we commonly measure test scores and exam results, mainly focused on cognitive skills, academic fields of knowledge and end-of-course assessments which are significantly a test of memory. Are these the right output measures for a knowledge-based economy using twenty-first-century technology? Should we, and if so can we, measure learning and competence in more appropriate ways? Should we, and if so can we, measure the wider output from schools which have promoted learning and other improvements beyond the students on roll?

- **The measurement of outcomes:** a primary reason behind our communal support for a public education service appears to be a widespread belief that in addition to personal benefits from learning and qualifications there are also major social benefits. *'Education is one of the most important predictors – usually, in fact, the most important predictor – of many forms of political and social engagement –'* (Helliwell and Putnam, 2007: 1). Many schools, including those in the PV enquiry want to contribute to outcomes such as social and emotional well-being, behaviour over lifetime, civility and community cohesion. There is good reason to believe that schools in England can make that contribution even though these less tangible and often longer-term outcomes are more difficult to measure and to account for (Campbell, 2006; OECD, 2006; Riddell, 2006).

- **The measurement of processes**: in schools the main process for transforming inputs into outputs is teaching and learning. The quality of teaching is key in the learning outcomes. In her final report, HMCI Christine Gilbert reported that *'Inadequate teaching [4%], is the exception rather than the rule, a far cry from the concerns reported by inspectors in pre-Ofsted days in around one third of the lessons seen'* (Ofsted, 2010a). The Ofsted criteria for judging teaching, which have their critics, nonetheless provide a snapshot of classroom performance. Systemically, in contrast, there are no suitable measures for the processes by which many school staff, including those in the PV enquiry, connect learning and other outcomes across age groups and across communities. These processes are not confined to observable classroom behaviours and they are less predictable, more diffuse. Setting measures for these processes is deeply problematic.

- **Determining timescales**: the timescales for delivery by schools operate to rhythms of national politics which never exceed five years and usually work to much shorter annual or bi-annual sequences. If welcome results from initiatives are not available in those kinds of timeframe then the span of political concentration wavers. Schools that under-perform immediately come under pressure to improve or to close. Effective improvement programmes are designed to deliver swift results in terms of exams. The pay offs from the kind of work in which the PV schools were engaged work to a different rhythm and may not be apparent for some time after students, families or communities have engaged in them. Activities like those sponsored by the PV schools can often only have an impact over a much longer period.

- **Selecting units of measurement**: the units of measurement for schools are pupils, lessons and exams. The units of measurement for the system in England are individual schools. These become like units in a production line – identifiable and distinct elements – but in a production line which is not self-contained or linear and whose complex lateral and horizontal connections are insufficiently acknowledged. The behaviour of communities, families and students has an effect on outcomes and outputs for schools. The reverse is also true. Less well acknowledged is the effect which schools can have on one another. There is some recognition of that effect in the managerial models of federations and chains now favoured by national policy makers (DfE, 2010d: 12 and Ch 5) and in which the leadership of several schools is invested in one person. That approach seems to be more about the effect of individual personalities across the piece rather than of institutions on one another. The reciprocal effect of neighbouring schools may be a 'zero sum game' for the neighbourhood overall but can have a dramatic effect on the fortune of the schools. 'Cream-skimming' and/or the subtle manipulation of parental preferences can cause the reallocation groups of well-disposed students away from lower-ranked schools (Adnett and Davies, 2003: 394). Current accountability systems mask the outcomes of interconnection – even of intended partnerships – from the schools' stakeholders (Hargreaves, 2011: 23). The projects profiled in the public value enquiry were developing relationships and networks between schools, other providers, families and communities. To properly account for that kind of work we need new forms of accountability to supplement the tight focus on individual school performance. Ainscow *et al.* (2012) suggest three.

○   *The unit of action* – focused on issues in an administratively defined area.

○   *Geographical and social boundaries* – focused on issues in an area that has clear physical boundaries, for example, main roads, or cultural boundaries such as a housing estate.

○   *Issues* – the focus on a particular issue, such as poor school attendance or teenage gang membership across geographical boundaries.

The challenge with all of this is how to attribute the outcome to the particular activity. Of course this matters not a jot to the community… but will be required more and more as we move further into a world of commissioning and integrated provision.
Margaret Nowell, Headteacher, St Thomas's Centre Pupil Referral Unit

Is the light worth the candle?

Is the effort these school leaders put into their innovative work, promoting community cohesion and creating public value, justified by the difference it makes to children and young people? If some of this work is a distraction which adds nothing to outputs or outcomes or worse, detracts from some, then it is better left alone.

There is a strand in the research canon which suggests that work by schools to involve parents and communities in support of children's learning does pay a dividend – though there are some gaps in that work which would benefit from further and better focused enquiry (Goodall and Vorhaus, 2010). Two summaries from different kinds of research review confirm that support and connections organised in the ways which we observed and reported to have been adopted by the PV leaders were likely to be successful. Harris and Goodall (2009: 20) described that successful initiatives were likely to include:

•   multi-dimensional interventions and delivery modes that address more than one facet of children's lives and meet the needs of a wide range of users
•   investment in high-quality staff training and qualifications, including volunteers

- locally-driven provision based on consultation and involvement of parents and local communities
- a focus on implementation factors.

O'Mara *et al.* (2010: 54) identified similar key factors for success:

- using joined-up, multi-agency approaches
- having a quality workforce
- using media to engage hard-to-reach people
- using both practical and therapeutic interventions simultaneously.

Leaders in the public value enquiry were both intuitive and informed in their commitment to wider and non-conformist working practice. They were unequivocal about the central importance of outputs and outcomes for young people and about the value of understanding cause and effect in their work. They believe that attainment and well-being are inextricably linked and that activity benefiting one contributes to the other. They felt deeply frustrated that some of what they think are vital outcomes continue to be regarded as less important than other outputs. They suspected that ease of measurement and numerical presentation give attainment outputs greater status than outcomes – a view that applied above all to statutory attainment targets – even when the latter are arguably an essential contribution to the former. At the heart of this matter is the debate about whether the output measures are sensitive enough to detect substantive differences in service quality or whether, in their current form, they obscure influential variations in input, not least variations in student background. For the PV leaders this debate turns on issues of equity and justice, which would not deny the central importance of attainment as an aide to ambition and social mobility for young people from relatively poor backgrounds. They would, however, challenge the dominance that attainment measures have, to the virtual exclusion of almost anything else, as a measure of school and education service performance. These arguments were recently summarised by colleagues from Manchester University's Centre for Equity in Education (Ainscow *et al.*, 2012). We share their conclusion that the equity issues which have dominated policy rhetoric, if not policy making, for the past two or three decades do not arise initially at the level of the individual school and cannot, therefore, be solved by intervention only at that level. What happens within schools, Ainscow and his colleagues say, is inextricably linked with what happens between and beyond schools. They describe a division within the international research community (which they might have added is reflected in some policy debates). On the one hand are those who argue that a school-focused approach is required, based on what is known about the most effective and improving schools in disadvantaged areas. On the other hand, there are those who argue that the inequalities are so profound, even before children enter schools, that despite some individual exceptions schools systemically cannot overcome that gap. This is a paradox eloquently summarised by Stephen Ball:

> *The over-whelming focus of education policy…..on 'raising standards' has done very little and perhaps can do no more to close performance outcome gaps between social class groups. I am not saying that standards have not been raised (whatever that might mean and whatever value in terms of public good that might deliver) but that performance gaps in terms of social class remain enormous… My point is that if we want to understand and explain persistent educational inequalities and do something about them through policy, then increasingly, the school is the wrong place to look and the wrong place to reform – at least in isolation from other sorts of changes in other parts of society.*
>
> (Ball, 2010:156 quoted in Ainscow *et al.*, 2012)

This is not a problem confined to England or the UK, it is an international phenomenon. The OECD's report on equity in education concluded that, despite significant expansion in education across the globe *'overall social mobility has not risen and in some places inequalities of income and wealth have increased'* (OECD, 2010d: 1). One of the 10 key recommendations made by the OECD *'which would help reduce school failure and dropout rates, make society fairer and help avoid the large social costs of marginalised adults with few basic skills'* (ibid.) was to strengthen the links between home and school. Schools, the OECD concludes, have a role to play in building *'effective relationships'* with students' homes, encouraging participation and support from parents and helping to develop home environments conducive to learning. On average 20 per cent of the organised learning time for children in the OECD, including homework, takes place outside the school (ibid.: 5). PV leaders and many others would endorse those sentiments in English contexts and then point out that so long as that aspect of their work passes without recognition, or is even seen as irrelevant, then its application will be limited and insecure. The challenge for those of us interested in work of this kind is to find a medium which allows us to describe its outcomes and outputs in a compelling account.

Data for measuring high status, nationally and institutionally authorised outputs is readily available. Every publicly funded school in England has access to tools like RAISEonline (RAISE, 2011) and the Fischer Family Trust data (FFT, 2011). These sources generate detailed analyses of the attainment and progress of pupils across each Key Stage, allowing comparison according to a wide range of contextual data including school size and, for pupils, numbers of boys and girls, their ethnic background, special needs, care arrangements, free school meal entitlement, absence levels and attainment at the previous point of national assessment. This data, along with data about attendance, the rate of exclusions and students' socio-economic circumstances is also collated and published nationally (DfE, 2011e). This material has been designed to allow each school to account for the first of the five capacity-building tasks we described in Chapter 5 – ensuring that teaching and learning deliver high level academic attainment. Beyond the first task, and beyond national and institutionally authorised outputs, explanation, justification and accountability become increasingly difficult. Establishing direct links between particular extra-curricular activities and desired outcomes – even if known outcomes are desired – becomes more and more tenuous. The fifth key task, making resources available as the basis for community activities which have no obvious direct or indirect payback, may on many occasions become little more than an act of faith. Even if it is supported by a combination of personal, associate and contextual authorisation and capacity, the fifth task – like most other innovative activity – is nevertheless out on a limb in so many ways. A local focus on effort and outcomes which are not officially authorised also raises questions about which non-statutory outcomes for young people are important and what consideration, if any, should be given by schools to improved outcomes for adults.

The leaders in the public value enquiry were asked to reflect on and to offer suggestions about these issues. Two proposals were made to stimulate the group's thinking and conversation. The first proposal was that a results-based accountability framework of the kind promoted by Mark Friedman might be a guide to gathering impact information, in particular asking the 'so what?' question (Friedman, 2005). Friedman proposed, in broad terms, that too many public service programmes tend to focus on delivery above impact. Means then become ends and, if the process is completed and the service delivered, boxes can be ticked as to whether or not it has made any difference for users and taxpayers. Friedman's proposal is that a tighter focus on ends will always be more productive; that it is important to know at the outset what the intended change for the user is and how that will be measured and reported. If the 'so what?' question cannot be answered then the value of a public programme cannot be explained, either to users or to taxpayers. The PV leaders found the four dimensions – effort, effect, quantity and quality – and the three associated questions in Table 6.1 below useful as a framework for discussing how impact could be explored and would recommend them to others.

Table 6.1: Framework for discussing impact

	Quantity	Quality
Effort	How much did we do?	How well did we do it?
Effect	Is anyone better off?	

Source: DCSF (2008b:12)

In conversation, the PV leaders commented on how often, especially with activity outside the classroom or school, they and their peers were drawn into occupying the top left quadrant of Table 6.1: 'How much did we do?'. This usually involved reporting that *'endless activities listed in action plans had been completed'* (as one leader described it) and hoping that evidence of effort was a virtue in its own right. The leaders were confident that they were occupying the top right hand quadrant some of the time and therefore beginning to address some of the 'How well did we do it?' questions. To do that they used measures of service quality and user satisfaction to which we will return later. The final and, in every sense, central question, 'Is anyone better off?' provoked a wide ranging debate about how it was possible to know and what constituted good evidence. This led to the second proposal: that numeric data is not the only or necessarily the best way of describing progress and development – narrative accounts also have their place and validity. This is not an intuitive position for an education service dominated by numeric analysis. We don't underestimate the value of numeric analysis but recurring themes from comparable and properly constructed narrative accounts also have validity in their own right.

What emerged from the leaders' conversation, enquiry and sharing of evidence was a strong confirmation of four points.

- Schools working in innovative ways and so creating public value can and do deliver good results on their core compact for good teaching and learning.
- It is helpful to be clear from an early stage in any initiative which extends beyond the core of teaching and learning just what the activity is meant to achieve, what its success criteria might be, how it will be recorded and how the reporting of progress and outcomes will enhance rather than strangle the activity.
- The cost benefit of effort and impact is harder to describe the more the activity and outcomes depend on factors outside the school's control.
- There are ways of reporting impact outside the statutory framework.

We have selected some examples of the schools' successes to illustrate those points although there is not enough space here to acknowledge all their achievements. We will also have to skim over the considerable effort required from the schools to reach these levels: *en route*, all have had their ups and downs. We will report on the traditional, statutory evidence of success recorded in Ofsted reports and end of Key Stage assessments before reporting on other success criteria that the schools shared with us – often in narrative form.

School improvement has to be your driver. Education provides the keys to the kingdom and every child deserves a set.
Sir Paul Edwards, Headteacher, Garforth Community College

We start, though, with evidence of what a struggle it can be. Early in this second phase of the public value enquiry, one of the schools, George Green's, had a disappointing Ofsted judgement and a notice to improve. Its end of Key Stage 4 results are now close to local authority and national averages. The inspection, that removed the notice after only a year, described the school overall as satisfactory and rapidly improving. It graded the following features of the school as good:

- the pupils' contribution to the school and wider community
- the extent to which the curriculum meets pupils' needs, including, where relevant, through partnerships
- the effectiveness of care, guidance and support
- the effectiveness of partnerships in promoting learning and well-being and
- the effectiveness with which the school promotes community cohesion.

The school considers these threads of its work to be vital – and never more so than in contributing to and sustaining its improvement from a temporary set back.

Ofsted judgements have been a source of affirmation for the impact of schools in the public value enquiry both in the classroom and with their communities. The following are quotes extracted from inspections at the other sites which took place during or since the enquiry. They demonstrate unequivocally that if it is not possible to prove directly that community connections enhance every aspect of school outputs and outcomes, it is possible to show that high attainment, good student well-being and strong community cohesion are very compatible.

- **Brixham Community College** *'...is a good and improving school [which] provides an outstanding level of care, advice and guidance for groups of students and for individuals by working closely with a range of outside agencies and education and business partners.'* The students' contributions to the life of the college and the wider community are described as extensive and outstanding thanks to the curriculum and the range of partnerships. The way the college has used creative media aspects of its visual arts specialism to work in tandem with the local fishing community in preserving its heritage is a great example of that.
- **The Castle Nursery School**, a part of the wider Children's Centre is outstanding and *'provides children with memorable first experiences that set them firmly on the path to lifelong learning'.* The leaders *'leave no stone unturned in an ongoing effort to engage as many people from the local community as possible [and] the school provides a haven for parents and community members who seek support'.*

- **Clifton Green Primary School** *'provides an outstanding education for its pupils with superb equality of opportunity for all'.* Its partnerships with other schools, wider children's services, local businesses and local communities are a celebratory thread running through its full Ofsted report. Its 2010 theme inspection described the school's English achievement and curriculum as *'outstanding'* and made direct reference to the *'distinctive and compelling reasons'* that the school's networks create for writing.
- **Coleshill Heath Primary School** is *'a good school where the care, support and guidance for pupils are outstanding'.* Its extended services make the school *'a focal point for the local community, which is rightly proud of its development in recent years'.*
- **Delaware Community Primary School** is *'an outstanding school [with] a wide range of major strengths'.* Its pupils make *'an outstanding contribution to the community through the many responsibilities they take on in school and through activities in the wider community…'*
- **Garforth Green Lane Primary School**, a member of the Garforth Partnership Trust, was graded an *'outstanding'* school where *'first rate partnerships with parents, other schools and the local community secure the school's reputation as a key neighbourhood asset'.*
- **St Thomas's Centre Pupil Referral Unit** *'is an outstanding PRU which deserves its excellent reputation with parents, carers and the community.'* Its personal social health and economic (PSHE) programme has been praised by Ofsted for actively involving pupils in community activities. The school is *'a highly inclusive community'* where the leadership has built successful links which benefit both the students and the local community and where expertise is readily shared through partnerships with local schools.
- **Swanlea** was described as *'an outstanding school where students of all abilities and backgrounds thrive, both academically and personally.'* Its students were said to have a *'strong sense of responsibility to the local communities'* and *'enrichment for the community provides very good access to a range of learning resources and activities …'*
- **Westwood Secondary School** is a good school, a *'friendly and safe place'* which is *'improving strongly'.* Most pupils make good progress compared to their often well-below-average prior attainment. The school is described as outstanding for the contribution its pupils make to the school and wider community and also for the effectiveness with which it promotes community cohesion.

The PV schools also have a good record to show in end of Key Stage results. In 2009 and 2010 all of the enquiry schools reported statutory end of Key Stage results that were well above floor targets. Two of the primary schools and two of the secondary schools had reported contextual value added (CVA) scores that were significantly above average. All the primary schools had results better than national and local authority averages; four of the five secondary schools had percentages below the national average for GCSE 5A*–C including English and maths but showed improvement above national average rates over the period of the enquiry (2008–10). All the PV leaders believe these figures would have been poorer if they were not engaged so closely with their communities and other services. Their work with particular vulnerable groups is repeatedly above national norms. The record of these schools on core attainment is positive and secure: so are there also collateral benefits accruing from the activity associated with public value?

The answer is that strong threads of positive impact and improved outcomes are discernible among the young people and communities served by these schools. The challenge is that the further these outcomes are removed from numeric measures collated by education, social care, health, youth justice and other children's services, the more difficult they are to describe in absolute terms and to attribute directly to the four key capacity-building tasks beyond the core of teaching and learning. In many cases, the schools turn to narratives as a way of reporting the link between improvements and activity beyond the classroom. The narrative form is, of course, susceptible to reporter bias but does put an account of the work into the public domain. Once there it can at least be scrutinised and tested by those with governance or other stakeholder interests in the work.

The public value enquiry certainly suggests that narrative could be a powerful tool alongside others in the development of self-improving systems. Part of the dynamic for that may be in the intrinsic value of the particular medium selected for the purposes of accountability. Whatever its content and irrespective of whether it is a numeric or narrative form, the fundamental value of new measures appears to be in the effect of the conversations, communications and connections which are needed to decide what they should be. The more open those are, the greater the demand to be clear about what are the desired ends and about whether the form of accountability is faithful to those ends. Below we divide the 'collateral outcomes' from the PV school into two broad groups: impact outcomes and process outcomes.

Impact outcomes

In broad terms, impact outcomes are evident when schools can report accredited, validated attainment. Attendance, behaviour both inside and no less importantly outside the school, higher levels of students leaving education to enter employment or training, reductions in teenage pregnancy or even accreditation of staff learning and development have been positive indicators which the PV schools have been able to associate with their wider activity.

Attendance was one of the more readily measurable areas of improvement that the enquiry schools referred to when celebrating the impact of their public value work. Sometimes it was associated with a particular activity, such as the pre-school and family support activities which have provided Coleshill Heath Primary School with the best attendance figures in its borough and sometimes it was associated with a particular group of pupils, like the previously persistent absentees at The Westwood Secondary School. Building commitment from families could be associated with those families taking their children's attendance more seriously.

Improvements in behaviour in school and even in the locality were also tracked by the schools. Clifton Green Primary School used a friendship survey as a formative assessment of pupils' sense of right and wrong. The school can also point to reports from the community and other services of the dramatic reduction in criminal damage locally, not least to school premises, the local youth club and the community space. The improvement can be tracked from the school's frustration with criminal damage on and around its site. The then headteacher called a community meeting and began to facilitate, but determinedly not chair or manage, community partnerships and cohesive activities. Other reported crime and antisocial behaviour also decreased in the neighbourhood. Anyone with knowledge of the northern tradition of 'mischief night' on 4 November will understand the school's pride that its area, in contrast with other areas in York, made no call on emergency services in 2009. Maps and tables produced for the school by the local police force demonstrate that very clearly and provide powerful evidence for the community cohesion element of the Ofsted inspection.

Trust status had nurtured a sense of commercial enterprise at Garforth which was having a positive effect on the number of young people not in employment, education or training (NEETs). More than 200 students attend the trust-owned hair and beauty salon, while the trust's construction facility has deployed students to renovate a newly acquired shop selling school uniform and equipment on Main Street, Garforth.

George Green's Secondary School and The Westwood Secondary School both associate their community relationships with improved student behaviour in school. Both also used local crime statistics to show how their neighbourhoods were improving compared with others in the same police area. George Green's could track outcomes for its students in nationally recognised qualifications within its youth service provision and knew that they were above target. Its Island Sports Trust (IST) supported progression from voluntary to employed work and the 25 young people who had worked for the IST in the previous five years have moved on to university or full-time employment.

St Thomas's Centre Pupil Referral Unit, which offers education to pregnant teenagers, has data to show the longer-term impact of its work: that no child of a local teenage mother in the past 20 years has been permanently excluded from mainstream provision, or been referred as a teenage parent themselves.

The Healthy Schools Award and Gold Arts Mark are also indicators of good outcomes. All of the leaders say their public value work generates interest and enthusiasm amongst their staff and nowhere was this clearer than at Delaware Community Primary School where five staff including the headteacher recently completed Master's degrees. Given, on one hand, the weakness of league tables as an indicator of future quality (Leckie and Goldstein, 2011; Gray *et al.*, 1999) and, on the other hand, the powerful association between continuing professional development, teacher quality and student attainment (Robinson *et al.*, 2009), families and communities might be better advised to ask schools about their in-service programmes than about their end of Key Stage results.

Process outcomes

> *Keep hold of the wider picture and perspective. View learning in the widest sense and view it as long term. Too many schools have structures in place that lead to goals that we don't really believe in, hurdles that we have to jump through. Don't lose sight of what learning really is about.*
>
> Jo Grail, formerly Headteacher Delaware Community Primary School

In broad terms, process outcomes are evident when schools can report that activities are in place, parents and communities are engaged and there is a reasonable expectation that, more or less directly, this will lead to impact outcomes for young people.

Clifton Green Primary School's partnership groups and Coleshill Heath Primary School's experience of parents around the site with their children an hour or more before school starts have not been achieved easily, but both believe the effort is paying dividends in terms of community engagement. They hope that engagement will result in increased aspiration and improved pupil outcomes. Coleshill Heath is now using the tracking system from the PE, School Sport and Young People (PESSYP) strategy to show how all of its pupils are involved in activity outside the school day.

Clifton Green and Coleshill Heath were also schools which used narrative forms as a regular medium for accountability. In the autumn term 2009, evaluation of its nurture group Clifton Green told the story of the work – the creation of a nurturing environment, the development of positive relationships, improved liaison between staff (including specialists) and better behaviour in the nurture class, across the school and at home – in two concise pages of text and four photographs. The work at Coleshill School and across the local authority, Solihull, has been celebrated in a case study published by the Training and Development Agency (TDA, 2010) which focused on Coleshill's work to improve attendance and attainment through employing a Family Support Worker. Delaware Primary is another whose development over the past few years has been captured in case studies involving 'new models of leadership' (Mongon and Chapman, 2009) and published on the National College website.

St Thomas's Centre Pupil Referral Unit creates narrative accounts of the wide range of tasks it undertakes with parents. By modelling positive behaviours through managing money, good eating habits, showing manners, washing laundry, being respectful, making and keeping appointments and paying attention to school work, it strives to build social capacity and to empower parents to take responsibility for their lives, and the lives of their children.

The Westwood Secondary School is just one of the schools that uses student surveys to highlight the impact of engagement with community groups and activities on changing student views and perceptions. Feedback from the surveys shows that the majority of students now have a deeper understanding of cultural diversity and community issues.

A comment from Garforth Community College summarised how difficult the question of impact can be and what motivates these leaders:

> We know from what families tell us that we are making a difference to their lives in many ways but we have little hard evidence yet to prove this. We know, for instance the crime has reduced in the area, but we have no hard and fast figures. We know that the emotional and mental health of some of our more vulnerable young people is improving, but we have no figures. We believe that the health of the community is improving but we are a long way off proving it. We are motivated by the anecdotal feedback we get from families.
>
> Paul Hirst, Garforth Schools Partnership Trust

The school is currently grappling with the challenge of establishing a causal link between attainment and its strong uniform policy and commercial acquisition of the town centre retail facility in order to deliver uniforms.

> We will not spend endless time proving direct correlation, but the children and families tell us that it makes them feel more ready for school and attaining high. It seems to raise aspirations all round…
>
> Paul Hirst, Garforth Schools Partnership Trust

Chapter 7

Conclusion

Understanding educational innovation

Industries that operate at mass scale work with dominant designs which allow for efficient, large-scale production; specialisation and a division of labour within and between organisations; standardisation of outputs and interfaces between organisations (Nooteboom, 2000).

Education in England and many other industrialised countries has clearly become such an industry. The dominant design of the school is not just the chief means to deliver learning; it also defines the output. Education is virtually synonymous with going to school.

A lot of learning and improvement, innovation even, can go on within dominant designs as individuals or small groups work out how to do things better. But how does a whole industry learn how to do new things and even realise that new products and services might be needed?

That is a vital question for all modern education systems and the schools profiled in this book provide the starting point for an answer. They also show that the process of innovation is often potentially, if not visibly, conflictual. Innovators working within systems that become increasingly focused on controlling performance have to be especially skilful and motivated to create the space in which they can innovate. To avoid outright conflict with the system of which they are a part, innovative leaders have to find ways to strike compromises, avoid attracting excessive attention and borrow resources relatively informally.

Modern school systems, especially in the developed world, are in danger of being caught between two very different approaches as they attempt to improve outcomes for all children, particularly those from poorer households.

One approach, often favoured by politicians and policy-making civil servants, but also supported, in the US at least, by some foundations and charter schools, is to focus on teaching and learning as the chief route to improving outcomes for children. This approach, favoured by many school reformers, is to focus on better teaching, on national tests and on following a national curriculum, with clear accountability for results. With better teachers who are better managed and held to account, results should improve across the board and variations due to social class, income, and locality should be reduced. One response to the stubborn failure of the education system to deliver equity is to make it even more systematic and unforgiving of deviations from the standard script.

Another response is to focus on the social background and conditions in which children are brought up. Demography is still destiny for too many children: where they are born and the income and occupations of their parents determine the kind of education they are likely to receive, the make-up and funding of the schools they go to. Too many children from less advantaged backgrounds do not get the high quality teaching and learning they deserve. This is an international phenomenon and, in the US – as Linda Darling Hammond describes for example – too many children from African-American and Latino backgrounds will find themselves in poor, highly socially segregated schools, with relatively inexperienced teachers, offering them fairly unexciting lessons (Hammond, 2010). Unless school reform is allied to measures to support more disadvantaged families and communities then demography will continue to determine destiny.

The PV school leaders profiled in this book are trying to find a way to reconcile elements of these two contrasting approaches. They recognise the pivotal role that school can play in the lives of the children they teach. They also recognise that innovation within school, to devise more effective and engaging forms of learning, will be key to closing the attainment gap. In other words their moral commitment to innovation and greater equity go hand in hand: the route to greater equity lies in innovations in education which mean that children from very different backgrounds, with different abilities and outlooks can each have exciting and engaging opportunities to learn. But in addition they realise they cannot be immune, or indifferent to the community from which their children and parents come. The PV schools see that their job will become easier the more effectively they engage with their community and their community will benefit from more engagement with a school that provides a measure of stability to localities where there are few large, stable, collective organisations – such as companies, churches or trade unions.

These PV leaders might be outliers, but then, as Charlie Leadbeater records in his descriptions of radical, pioneering education opportunities created in cash-poor areas across the world (Leadbeater, 2012), it is true that most non-incremental innovation comes from outside mainstream systems and markets. Dominant designs evolve through the creation of novel combinations, usually incorporating old and familiar routines and practices with new and borrowed ones.

Schooling was once itself a successful innovation and like other innovations, as it becomes consolidated, it starts to spread and diffuse. In the nineteenth and early twentieth-century people demanded more and better schools because they were seen to be successful. As a dominant design diffuses into new contexts it meets new challenges which expose the limitations of the original design. A design that works in one setting may not in another. If the process of diffusion is lengthy, as it has been with schools, then the context may change: an innovation designed to educate the industrial working class operates less successfully or to outdated expectations when the economy has become largely driven by innovation and services. As a result the dominant design has to learn and adapt and it usually does so by adopting new combinations, preserving elements of current practice but drawing in ingredients from neighbouring practices and finding a new organisational architecture to blend them together.

This process of creating new combinations to meet new challenges lies at the heart of most innovation. Take the evolution of sailing ships in the fifteenth to eighteenth centuries. The triangular sail favoured by Portuguese and Arab sailors allowed for much greater manoeuvrability, especially sailing into the wind, and so was good for ships entering and leaving rivers and ports. The square sail favoured by Northern Europeans was good for sailing fast with the wind. It became apparent when risk-taking individuals stepped outside the two cultural expectations and tested the prototypes, that a multi-masted sailing ship, which incorporated both types of sail, would perform better than either. Another example of this process of innovation through the combination of reciprocal ideas from different sources is the windmill, which combines the sail from ships for wind power, and the shaft, gears and transmission from watermills.

The schools profiled in this report are part of just such a process, one that is familiar to other industries. Adapting the account of this process set out by Bart Nooteboom, the historian and theorist of innovation based at Erasmus University in Rotterdam, this is how we can understand the process of educational innovation and the role of the PV schools in that process (Noteboom, 2000).

The consolidation of the dominant design for schools takes place in the late nineteenth and early twentieth centuries. From the early twentieth century onwards political and economic pressures led to the diffusion of that dominant design so that more children spent longer in school. Yet as the standard model was diffused to different contexts and as the contexts it operated in changed, its limitations were exposed. That triggered a search for more effective solutions, initially within the key parameters of the basic design: raising school leaving ages, introducing and abandoning selection at 11+, tinkering with the curriculum and assessment, introducing new technologies. The limitations proved to be stubborn and therefore policy makers turned to new combinations of reciprocal services, for example blending education for children with family support services for parents. Eventually some of this tinkering and some of the new combinations have gelled. They have found a sustainable organisational form. They, in turn and in some places if not universally, may become a new dominant design which operates as an alternative to the original. In new technology and communications industries, such as web-based services, this cycle can be rapid, lasting little more than a year. In education the cycle moves at glacial pace, it is extended over decades – perhaps, we can now wonder, even over centuries. In particular the gap between a new combination being invented and a new organisational form emerging to exploit that invention can be very long. That is because it often takes people a long time to be able to incorporate new ideas into existing routines, to see the value and point of an innovation. If a new invention is so novel that it can hardly be understood then it will remain an interesting oddity. To be adopted an idea has to be novel enough to bring change but not so novel it cannot be understood. It took more than three centuries before the submarine developed from prototype to an effective vehicle for naval warfare when it was able to borrow ideas from modern shipbuilding and engines.

This process of innovation, however, only gets started if, as a dominant model diffuses, local practitioners have the means and the incentives to respond to local need that does not fit the dominant model. Exploitation of the benefits of the standard approach requires control, coordination, consistency and a degree of stability. Exploration for new approaches requires variety, looser control and a degree of plasticity in organisations. Fixity and flux, stability and plasticity are each in its place valuable contributors to innovation. That is why the task of leading organisations in the midst of this search for novel combinations is so hard: managers need to lead organisations into ambiguous and uncertain terrain where old recipes are no guarantee of effectiveness.

That is what these brave school leaders are doing: they are prepared to acknowledge that the dominant design for education – the 'standalone' school – is not effective in their working context, so they have set off in search of new reciprocal combinations of practices that may provide a more effective approach. As they have done so their schools have increasingly come to look – as windmills, multi-masted sailing ships, submarines and many ground-breaking inventions all initially did – like ungainly hybrids. They seek to be both nationally and locally accountable for test results and the social and emotional well-being of their families, by working in school and in their communities, delivering standardised services for people, and also working with them to devise solutions tailored to their needs as well as working with a workforce of teachers, supplemented by many other skills. They find themselves in a creative but ambiguous, and sometimes uncomfortable, place.

One measure of the progress they are making is the triangle of public service innovation we introduced in the introduction to this report with its connected ingredients:

- creating *new capacity* to provide new services and solutions
- a supportive *authorising environment*
- *measures of value* to guide the innovation process and underpin its legitimacy.

We are now in a clearer position to assess their progress on these three fronts and what more might be done to support them.

The first requirement is the authorising environment which makes innovation possible and shows that it is encouraged by those in positions of power and influence, locally and nationally. As we have noted, aspects of the national environment are becoming more supportive: the emphasis on more joined up solutions; a growing interest in the way public services generate social capital and work through social networks; the collaboration between education and children's services and the opportunity for increasingly autonomous schools to craft their own approach. Yet the environment is also complex. School leaders must be careful to manage their educational performance – standards and results – to make sure they do not lose local support or risk intervention from central government agencies. Locally the picture is just as complex and challenging. The task of leading these schools requires constant, careful management of relationships and partnerships with local stakeholders. It is considerably more complex and outward facing than leading a school that is solely focused on delivering good teaching and learning. Developing these leadership skills will be vital for the innovation to prosper but political leaders need to develop their support – to encourage the testing of locally based solutions to often chronic challenges.

On the second front, the PV schools have been making some progress in creating a new kind of capacity within the education system, a hybrid mix of school, family programmes and community development with outreach and social enterprise. This is not rocket science. It is mainly a question of creating new ways to work based on combining existing approaches. Few if any of the ingredients are new. The recipe to combine them is new and full of vitality. However to take this forward, to build capacity into a sustainable and repeatable model, more work will have to be done to explore new roles and skills, for example the role of a community-based teacher or parent mentor – building on the *ad hoc* solutions these schools have so far been able to devise.

The final ingredient in our triangle is measurement of value. It is difficult to build a case for innovation, to select promising ideas and develop them, unless innovators have constant feedback. (One of the features of innovations on the web is the rapidity of feedback, for example in responses on Facebook or the way Google provides search results.) The schools profiled here clearly find this a very problematic area of their work. They are largely flying blind. They are not specialists in measurement of value. They sense they are adding value and can attest impressive qualitative measures and anecdotes. But systematic measures of the wider social value that they believe is important are not readily available to them. It is too reductive to reduce all their wider efforts in the community simply to the impact on test scores. Schools need help with measuring what they want to understand about the wider outcomes of their work. The alternative is that they, along with the agencies and communities to which they want to be responsible, will be comparing apples and pears in terms of their inputs, outputs, achievements and processes endlessly and (despite the metaphor) fruitlessly.

So while, overall, it would be fair to say that some of the elements needed to support this kind of innovation are falling into place, most – and in particular measurement of value – remain in development.

This causes us to consider a fourth ingredient, pulling the public value triangle into a diamond and making policy frameworks an explicit factor. It is difficult to see how these innovations will be sustained and spread unless there is a supportive national policy framework that allows them to flourish and to infiltrate the dominant design framework. Whether the previous Labour Government's policies were beginning to create such a supportive framework remains arguable and undecided. Whether the Coalition Government's policies for the education service, driving local autonomy and embracing the Big Society, will offer a supportive framework remains, at the time of writing, to be seen. Unless it does, then initiatives like those we are reporting will continue to be occasional and marginally influential rather than systemic and widely effective.

If we represented the four ingredients of innovation in a diamond with a weighted assessment of how far developed each ingredient is it might look like Figure 7.1. A perfectly successful innovation would score 100 per cent at each corner of the diamond and so total 400 per cent. Emphasising that we are thinking about how far school engagement with public value has come and not its potential, we would at the moment score it at a total of 170 per cent. Readers might pause for a moment to estimate their own sense of where the work is.

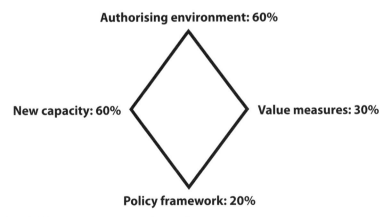

Figure 7.1: Public service innovation diamond

Reflecting on the value of the work of the PV schools has also allowed us to reflect on the different kinds of innovation strategies available to schools. Adapted from Leadbeater and Wong (2010) – see also Chapter 2 in this book – this is a consideration of whether the schools are engaged in technical or disruptive innovation, inside or outside the system and therefore whether they are improving, complementing, reinventing or transforming their field.

All schools are innovating and *improving* their current performance: this is technical innovation. These schools, however, are also seeking to innovate by *complementing* what schools traditionally do by adding other services. Some of these schools are also *reinventing* what it means to be a school, for example devising more personalised approaches to learning. They are not yet schools which are transforming how or where young people learn though, as is often the case with early stage innovation, the potential for transformation can be seen. Transformational innovation would radically change how and where learning takes place, challenging even the notion of the reinvented or supplemented school. It might, for example, make learning available in new ways in the community, outside school, perhaps not even involving teachers. Transformational innovation implies alternatives to school, not just alternative forms of school. That would mean PV schools eventually becoming something different: perhaps a network or a movement or a cultural programme or indeed a social enterprise, within which learning takes place. At the moment they are schools with add-on features which have created a new hybrid. In time the needs of their communities, families and pupils might best be served, however, by their becoming something different, for example social enterprises with a school at their heart.

Finally there is the vexed issue of scale. At the core of all these efforts is the idea that better learning outcomes and life chances stem from the combination of better schools and community development and family services. One of the most impressive examples of that principle operating at scale, across an entire community rather than in a single school, is the Harlem Children's Zone (HCZ) in New York which aims to transform the aspirations and achievements of a whole generation of 10,000 children living in 97 blocks in one of the most devastated urban communities in America (Dobbie and Fryer, 2009; Russell, 2009; HCZ, 2011). An 8-year-old boy in Harlem has a 33 per cent chance of ending up in prison. A third of students drop out of high school. Three-quarters of Harlem children cannot pass the grade exams for their age. The HCZ, inspired by community activist Geoffrey Canada, set out to mobilise family and peer support to encourage learning, to make going to college the norm and to break the culture of low aspirations. HCZ starts work with parents before their children are born. It offers pre-kindergartens, personal tutoring, dance and sports classes, food co-ops and social services help with housing and health issues. Five years after Canada opened his first academy, the *Harvard University Review*, in an article authored by Dobbie and Fryer, found the HCZ was *'enormously effective at raising the achievement level of the poorest minority of children'* (2009: 3). About 97 per cent of the Promise academy eighth-graders are performing at or above their grade. The Harlem Children's Zone has driven improvements in educational performance by linking what happens at school to what goes on outside it. The Obama administration is setting out to create a further 20 Promise Neighbourhoods, inspired by the HCZ model.

Radical innovations like the HCZ rarely start in the mainstream and usually take a long time to gestate before they are ready to diffuse and scale. Most often, radical innovation starts in the margins, where risk-averse incumbents fear to tread. Sometimes the margins infiltrate the mainstream but persuading incumbents to change their ways is often a thankless task. More often the margins find themselves pulling the mainstream in their direction because the solutions they have devised come to be seen as valuable. The margins become the new mainstream. Often that process can take a long time. Ideas can go out of fashion before being rediscovered. The first low cost airline was launched by Freddie Laker in the 1970s. Only in the last decade has that initial, failed, idea been turned into a winning formula all over the world. That may yet be what happens to the new public value model created by these schools.

References

Adnett, N. and Davies, P. (2003) Schooling reforms in England: from quasi-markets to competition? *Journal of Educational Policy*, Vol. 18, No. 4, 393–406.

Aho, E., Pitkänen, K. and Salhlberg, P. (2006) *Policy Development and Reform Principles of Basic and Secondary Education in Finland since 1968*, Working Paper Series: Education 2. Washington DC: World Bank.

Ainley, P. (2001) From a national system locally administered to a national system nationally administered: The new Leviathan in education and training in England. *Journal of Social Policy*, 30, 3, 457–76.

Ainscow, M., Dyson, A., Goldrick, S. and West, M. (2012) *Developing Equitable Education Systems*. London: Routledge.

Alexander, R., Rose, J. and Woodhead, C. (1992) *Curriculum Organisation and Classroom Practice in Primary Schools: A Discussion Paper*. London: DES.

Alford, J. and O'Flynn, J. (2009) Making sense of public value: Concepts, critiques and emergent meanings. *International Journal of Public Administration*, 32:3–4, 171–91.

Audit Commission (2005) *Governing Partnerships Bridging the Accountability Gap*. London: The Audit Commission.

Auld, R. (1976) *William Tyndale Junior and Infants Schools Public Inquiry: A report to the Inner London Education Authority, London 1976*. London: ILEA.

Baird, A., Haynes, J., Massey F. and Wild, R. (2010) *Public Service Output, Input and Productivity: Education*. London: Office for National Statistics.

Ball, S. J. (2008) *The Education Debate*. Bristol: Policy Press.

-- (2010) New class inequalities in education. *International Journal of Sociology and Social Policy*, 30 (3/4), 155–66.

Barber, M. and Mourshed, M. (2007) *How The World's Best Performing School Systems Come Out On Top*. London: McKinsey.

Barr, N. (undated) *The benefits of education: What we know and what we don't*. London: HM Treasury. Online http://www.hm-treasury.gov.uk/d/252.pdf (accessed 14 September 2011).

Becker, G.S. (1981) *A Treatise on the Family.* Cambridge MA: Harvard University Press.

Becker, G.S. and Tomes, N. (1986) Human capital and the rise and fall of families. *Journal of Labor Economics 4* (no 3, pt 2), S1–S39.

Benington, J. (2009) Creating the public in order to create public value? *International Journal of Public Administration*, 32:3–4, 232–49.

Bentley, T. (1998) *Learning Beyond the Classroom: Education for a changing world.* London: Routledge.

Blanchflower, D. and Oswald, A. (2000) Wellbeing over Time in Britain and the US. Paper presented at the National Bureau of Economic Research Summer Workshop in Cambridge Mass, July (2000). Online: http://www2.warwick. ac.uk/fac/soc/economics/staff/academic/oswald/julywellbeing2000.pdf (accessed 14 September 2011).

Blatchford, P., Russell A., and Webster R., (2012) *Reassessing the Impact of Teaching Assistants: How research changes practice and policy.* London: Routledge.

Blau, D.M. (2008) The effect of income on child development. *Review of Economics and Statistics*, 81(2), 261–76.

Blaug, R., Horner, L. and Lekhi, R. (2006) *Public value, politics and public management: A literature review.* London: The Work Foundation. Online: http://www.workfoundation.com/assets/docs/publications/117_politics_lit_ review.pdf (accessed 19 September 2011).

Burkard, T. and Clelford, T. (2010) *Cutting the Children's Plan: A £5 billion experiment gone astray.* London: Centre for Policy Studies.

Bynner, J. and Egerton, M. (2000) *The Wider Benefits of Higher Education.* London: Institute of Education, University of London. Online: http://www. hefce.ac.uk/pubs/hefce/2001/01_46.htm (accessed 14 September 2011).

Cabinet Office (2010) *Building The Big Society.* Online: http://www.cabinetoffice. gov.uk/news/building-big-society (accessed 15 September 2011).

Caldwell, B. (2008) Reconceptualizing the self-managing school. *Educational Management Administration Leadership*, 36: 235–49.

Campbell, D.E. (2006) What is education's impact on civic and social engagement? Presentation at the Symposium on Social Outcomes of Learning, held at the Danish University of Education. Online: http://www.oecd.org/ dataoecd/14/63/37425694.pdf (accessed 29 September 2011).

Christakis, N.A. and Fowler, J.H. (2010) *Connected: The surprising power of our social networks and how they shape our lives.* New York: Little, Brown and Company.

Close, P. and Wainwright, J. (2010) Who's in charge: leadership and culture in extended services. *School Leadership and Management,* Vol 30, no 5, 435–50.

Coleman, J.S., Campbell, E.Q., Hobson, C.J., McPartland, F., Mood, A.M. and Weinfeld, F.D. (1966) *Equality of educational opportunity.* Washington, DC: U.S. Government Printing Office.

Conger, K.J., Rueter, M.A. and Conger, R. (1999) The role of economic pressure in the lives of parents and their adolescents: The family stress model, in Crocket, L. (ed.) *Negotiating Adolescence in Times of Social Change.* Cambridge: Cambridge University Press.

Conway, D. (2010) *Liberal Education and the National Curriculum.* London: Civitas. Online: http://www.civitas.org.uk/pdf/LiberalEducation.pdf (accessed 3 September 2011).

Copland, M.A. (2003) Leadership of inquiry: Building and sustaining capacity for school improvement. *Educational Evaluation and Policy Analysis,* 25(4): 375–95.

Corbett, A. (1972) The school governors we want. *Where: The education magazine for parents,* 69, May/June. Quoted in Davis, J. (2002), op. cit.: 282.

Crabtree, J. (2004) The revolution that started in a library. *The New Statesman,* 17(826), 54–56, September 27. Online: http://www.newstatesman.com/200409270026 (accessed 27 November 2011).

Darling-Hammond, L. (2010) *The Flat World and Education: How America's commitment to equity will determine our future.* New York: Teachers College Press.

Day, C., Sammons, P., Hopkins, D., Leithwood, K. and Kington, A. (2008a) Research into the impact of school leadership on pupil outcomes: policy and research contexts. *School Leadership and Management,* 28(1): 5–25.

Day, C., Sammons, P., Hopkins, D., Harris, A., Leithwood, K., Gu, Q., Penlington, C., Mehta, P. and Kington, A. (2008b) *The impact of school leadership on pupil outcomes.* Nottingham: Department for Children, Schools and Families (Research Report DCSF – RR018). Online: https://www.education.gov.uk/publications/RSG/publicationDetail/Page1/DCSF-RR018 (accessed: 21 October 2011).

DCLG (2010) *The New Deal for Communities Experience: A final assessment.* London: Department for Communities and Local Government. Online: http://www.communities.gov.uk/publications/communities/afinalassessment (accessed on 27 September 2011).

DCSF (2007a) *The Children's Plan: Building brighter futures* (Cm 7280). London: The Stationery Office. Online: https://www.education.gov.uk/publications/standard/publicationDetail/Page1/CM%207280 (accessed on 21 September 2011).

-- (2007b) *Extended schools: building on experience.* London: DCSF. Online: www.dcsf.gov.uk/everychildmatters/_download/?id=1352 (accessed on 4 February 2010).

-- (2007c) *Guidance on the duty to promote community cohesion.* London: DCSF. Online: http://publications.teachernet.gov.uk/eOrderingDownload/DCSF-00598-2007.pdf (accessed on 21 September 2011).

-- (2008a) *Youth Cohort Study and Longitudinal Study of Young People in England: The activities and experiences of 16 year olds – England 2007.* London: DCSF. Online: www.dcsf.gov.uk/rsgateway/DB/SBU/b000795/index.shtml (accessed on 14 September 2011).

-- (2008b) *Better Outcomes for Children and Young People.* London: DCSF.

-- (2009a) *Breaking the Link Between Disadvantage and Low Attainment: Everyone's business.* Nottingham: DCSF.

-- (2009b) *Your Child, Your Schools, Our Future: Building a 21st century schools system* (Cm 7588). London: The Stationery Office. Online: http://publications.dcsf.gov.uk/eOrderingDownload/21st_Century_Schools.pdf (accessed 21 September 2011).

Dean, C., Dyson, A., Gallannaugh, F., Howes, A. and Raffo, C. (2007) *Schools, Governors and Disadvantage.* York: Joseph Rowntree Foundation.

Denhardt, R.B. and Denhardt, J.V. (2000) The New Public Service: Serving Rather Than Steering. *Public Administration Review*, Vol. 60, No. 6, 549–59.

DES (1977) *Education in Schools: A consultative document*, Green Paper Cmnd 6869. London: HMSO.

-- (1984) *Initial Teacher Training: Approval of courses*, Circular 3/84. London: DES.

-- (1989) *The National Curriculum: From policy to practice.* London: DES and Welsh Office.

DfE (2010a) *Powers to Facilitate Innovation Annual Report for the Academic Year Ending 31 July 2010.* London: The Stationery Office.

-- (2010b) *GCSE and Equivalent Attainment by Pupil Characteristics in England, 2009/10.* Online: http://www.education.gov.uk/rsgateway/DB/SFR/s000977/index.shtml (accessed on 14 October 2011).

-- (2010c) *Outcomes for Children Looked After by Local Authorities in England, as at 31 March 2010*. Online: http://www.education.gov.uk/rsgateway/DB/SFR/s000978/sfr38-2010v3.pdf (accessed on 27 September 2011).

-- (2010d) *The Importance of Teaching: The Schools White Paper 2010*. London: HMSO.

-- (2011a) *Press Notice*. Online: http://www.education.gov.uk/inthenews/inthenews/a0061085/gove-teachers-not-politicians-know-how-best-to-run-schools (accessed on 15 September 2011).

-- (2011b) (Department for Education) *Guidance on the Pupil Premium*. London: DfE. Online: www.thegrid.org.uk/info/welfare/.../guidance_pupil_premium_dfe.doc (accessed on 9 September 2011).

-- (2011c) *School Workforce in England, November 2010* (Provisional). London: DFE. Online http://www.education.gov.uk/rsgateway/DB/SFR/s000997/index.shtml (accessed on 22 September 2011).

-- (2011d) *About Academies*. London: DfE. Online: http://www.education.gov.uk/schools/leadership/typesofschools/academies/a0061252/about-academies (accessed on 21 September 2011).

-- (2011e) Research and Statistics Gateway. Online: http://www.education.gov.uk/rsgateway/index.shtml (accessed 29 September 2011).

DfEE (1998) *Standards for the Award of Qualified Teacher Status*. London: DfEE.

DfES (2005) *Extended schools: Access to opportunities and services for all – a prospectus*. Nottingham: DfES.

-- (2007) *Making Great Progress: Schools with outstanding rates of progression in Key Stage 2*. Nottingham: Department for Education and Skills. Online: https://www.education.gov.uk/publications/standard/publicationdetail/page1/DFES-00443-2007 (accessed on 21 October 2011).

Dobbie, W. and Fryer, R.G. Jr (2009) *Are High-Quality Schools Enough to Close the Achievement Gap? Evidence from a bold social experiment in Harlem*. Harvard University Working Paper w15473, April 2009. Online: www.nber.org/papers/w15473 (accessed 28 October 2011).

DoH (Department of Health) (2001) *Outcome Indicators for Looked After Children: Year ending 30 September 2000 – England*. Online: http://www.dh.gov.uk/prod_consum_dh/groups/dh_digitalassets/@dh/@en/documents/digitalasset/dh_4021781.pdf (accessed 22 July 2011).

Donnachie, I. (2000) *Robert Owen: Owen of New Lanark and New Harmony*. East Linton: Tuckwell Press.

Earley, P. (ed.) (1998) *School Improvement after Inspection.* London: Paul Chapman.

Earley, P. (2003) Leaders or followers? Governing bodies and their role in school leadership. *Educational Management and Administration*, vol. 31, no. 4, 353–367.

Earley, P. and Creese, M. (2003) Governors and school improvement. *Research Matters*, no. 20. London: Institute of Education, University of London.

Earley, P., Evans, J., Gold, A., Collarbone, P. and Halpin, D. (2002) *Establishing the Current State of School Leadership in England.* London: DfES.

Elder, G.H. and Caspi, A. (1988) Economic stress in lives: Developmental perspectives. *Journal of Social Issues,* 44(4), 25–45.

Feinstein, L. (2003) How Early Can We Predict Future Educational Achievement? Very Early. *CentrePiece*, Summer, 23–30.

Feinstein, L., Duckworth, K. and Sabates, R. (2004) *A model of inter-generational transmission of educational success.* London: Centre for Research on the Wider Benefits of Learning, Institute of Education, University of London. (Wider benefits of learning research reports: 10). Online: www.learningbenefits.net/ Publications/ResReps/ResRep10.pdf (accessed 21 October 2011).

Feldman, M.S. and Khademian, A.M. (2002) To manage is to govern. *Public Administration Review*, Vol. 62, No. 5, 541–54.

FFT (2011) Fischer Family Trust Data Analysis Project. Online: http://www. fischertrust.org/ (accessed 29 September 2011).

Fielding, M. (1999) Radical collegiality: Affirming teaching as an inclusive professional practice. *Australian Educational Researcher* 26(2), 1–34.

-- (2001) Students as radical agents of change, *Journal of Educational Change,* 2: 123–41.

-- (2006) Leadership, radical student engagement and the necessity of person-centred education, *International Journal of Leadership in Education*, Vol. 9, No. 4, 299–313

Flint, N. (2010) Schools, communities and social capital, unpublished research associate report produced by the headteacher of Aspinal Primary School, Manchester, for the National College.

Foucault, M. (1977) *Discipline and Punish: The birth of the prison.* London: Penguin.

Friedman, M. (2005) *Trying Hard is Not Good Enough.* Victoria, Canada: Trafford Publishing.

Fryer, R. and Levitt, S. (2004) Understanding the Black-White Test Score Gap in the First Two Years of School. *The Review of Economies and Statistics,* 86(2): 447–64.

Fullan, M. (2005) *Leadership and Sustainability: System thinkers in action.* California: Corwin.

Gardner, P. (2002) Teachers, in Aldrich, P. (ed.) *A Century of Education.* London: Routledge.

Goodall, J. and Vorhaus, J. (2010) *Review of Best Practice in Parental Engagement,* Research Report DFE-RR156. London: Institute of Education, University of London.

Goodman, A. and Gregg, P. (2010) *Poorer Children's Educational Attainment: How important are attitudes and behaviours?* York: Joseph Rowntree Foundation.

Gove, M. (2011) Michael Gove to the Education World Forum. Online: http://www.education.gov.uk/inthenews/speeches/a0072274/michael-gove-to-the-education-world-forum (accessed 19 September 2011).

Grace, G. (1995) *School Leadership: Beyond educational management – an essay in policy scholarship.* London: Routledge.

Gray, J., Hopkins, D., Reynolds, D., Wilcox, B., Farrell, S. and Jesson, D. (1999) *Improving Schools: Performance and Potential.* Buckingham: Open University Press.

Hanley, L. (2007) *Estates: An intimate history.* London: Granta.

-- (3 May 2011) Why northern children are playing dead at school. *The Guardian.* Online: http://www.guardian.co.uk/commentisfree/2011/may/03/academic-grades-northern-children (accessed 30 September 2011).

Hansard (1862) *House of Commons Debate 13 February 1862,* vol 165 para 228. Online: http://hansard.millbanksystems.com/commons/1862/feb/13/education-the-revised-code-o-regulations (accessed 1 September 2011).

-- (2010) *Education Committee 28th July 2010,* Question Numbers 60–72. Online: http://www.publications.parliament.uk/pa/cm201011/cmselect/cmeduc/395-i/395-i05.htm (accessed 21 September 2011).

Hanushek, E. (1998) *The Evidence on Class Size,* Occasional Paper, 98–1. Rochester, NY:Institute of Political Economy, University of Rochester.

Hargreaves, D. (2003) *Education Epidemic: Transforming secondary schools through innovation networks.* London: Demos.

-- (2010) *Creating a Self-improving School System.* Nottingham: National College. Online: http://www.nationalcollege.org.uk/docinfo?id=133672&filename=creating-a-self-improving-school-system.pdf (accessed 16 May 2011).

-- (2011) *Leading a Self-improving School System*. Nottingham: National College for School Leadership. Online: http://www.nationalcollege.org.uk/index/leadershiplibrary/leadingschools/working-in-partnership/school-to-school-support/leading-a-self-improving-school-system.htm (accessed 6 December 2011).

Harris, A, and Chapman, C. (2002) *Effective leadership in schools facing challenging circumstances*. Nottingham: NCSL.

Harris, A. and Goodall, J. (2009) *Helping Families Support Children's Success at School*. London: Save the Children.

Harris, A. and Spillane, J. (2008) *Distributed School Leadership: Developing tomorrow's leaders*. London: Routledge.

Hatcher, R. (2006) Social class and schooling: differentiation or democracy? In Cole, M. (ed.) *Education, Equality and Human Rights: Issues of gender, 'race', sexuality, disability and social class*. London: Routledge, 202–24.

Hautamäki, J., Harjunen, E., Hautamäki, A., Karjalainen, T., Kupiainen, S., Laaksonen, S., Lavonen, J., Pehkonen, E., Rantanen, P. and Scheinin, P. (2008) *PISA 06 Finland: Analyses, reflections and explanations*. Ministry of Education publications 2008:44. Online: http://www.pisa2006.helsinki.fi/files/PISA06_Analyses_Reflections_and_Explanations.pdf (accessed 14 October 2011).

HCZ (2011) *Changing the Odds*. New York: Harlem Children's Zone. Online: www.hcz.org (accessed 4 October 2011).

Heckman, J. (1995) Lessons from the bell curve. *Journal of Political Economics*, 103(5), 1091–1120.

Heckman, J., Stixrud, J. and Urzua, S. (2006) The effects of cognitive and noncognitive abilities on labor market outcomes and social behaviour. *Journal of Labor Economics*, 24(3), 411–82.

Heifetz, R. and Linsky, M. (2002) *Leadership on the Line*. Boston: Harvard Business School Press.

Helliwell, J.F. and Putnam, R.D. (2007) Education and social capital. *Eastern Economic Journal*, Vol. 33, No. 1, Winter. Online: http://wellbeing.econ.ubc.ca/helliwell/papers/Helliwell-Putnam-EEJ2007.pdf (accessed 28 September 2011).

Hills, J. and Stewart, K. (eds) (2005) *A More Equal Society? New Labour, poverty, inequality and exclusion*. Bristol: Policy Press.

HMSO (1977) *A New Partnership for Our Schools: Report of the Committee of Enquiry* (The Taylor Report). London: HMSO.

Huxham, C. and Vangen, S. (2005) *Managing to Collaborate: The theory and practice of collaborative advantage.* London: Routledge.

Innovation Unit (2009) *The Bridge Change Leadership Framework.* London: Innovation Unit. Online: http://www.innovationunit.org/knowledge/free-resources/toolkits/bridge-change-leadership-framework (accessed 21 October 2011).

Jackson, M. and Gretton, J. (1976) *William Tyndale: Collapse of a school – or a system?* London: Allen and Unwin.

James, C., Brammer, S., Conolly, M., Fertig, M., James, J. and Jones, J. (2010) *The 'Hidden Givers': A study of school governing bodies in England.* Reading: CfBT.

Keys, W. and Fernandes, C. (1990) *A Survey of Governing Bodies.* Slough: NFER.

Knight, B. (1993) Delegated financial management and school effectiveness, in Dimmock, C. (ed.) *School-based management and school effectiveness.* London: Routledge.

Lankinen, T. (Director General, Finnish National Board of Education) (2009) Presentation to Innovation in Education Conference, *Guardian*/Innovation Unit, November 9, 2009.

Leadbeater, C. (2008a) *What Next? 21 Ideas for 21st century learning.* London: Innovation Unit.

-- (2008b) *We-Think: Mass innovation not mass production.* London: Profile Books.

-- (2012) *Innovation in Education: Lessons from pioneers around the world.* London: Bloomsbury.

Leadbeater, C. and Mongon, D. (2008) *Leadership for Public Value: Achieving valuable outcomes for children, families and communities.* Nottingham: National College for School Leadership. Online: http://www.nationalcollege.org.uk/docinfo?id=17241andfilename=leadership-for-public-value.pdf (accessed 13 October 2011).

Leadbeater, C. and Wong, A. (2010) *Learning from the Extremes.* Amsterdam: Cisco.

Leana, C.R. (2011) The missing link in school reform. *Stanford Social Innovation Review*, Fall, 30–35.

Leckie, G. and Goldstein, H. (2011) A note on 'The limitations of school league tables to inform school choice'. *Journal of the Royal Statistical Society*: Series A (Statistics in Society) Volume 174, Issue 3, 833–36.

Leithwood, K., Mascall, B. and Strauss, T. (2008) *Distributed Leadership According to the Evidence.* London: Routledge.

Lexmond, J. and Reeves, R. (2009) *Building Character: Parents are the architects of a fairer society*. London: Demos.

Lord, P., Hart, R., Martin, K. and Atkinson, M. (2009) *Narrowing the Gap in Outcomes: Governance* (LGA Research Report). Slough: NFER.

MacBeath, J. (2008) Distributed leadership: paradigms, policy, and paradox, in Leithwood, K. Mascall, B. and Strauss, T. (eds) *Distributed Leadership According to the Evidence*. London: Routledge.

Maddison, A. (2001) *The World Economy: A millennial perspective*. Paris: OECD.

McKinsey (2009) *The Economic Impact of the Achievement Gap in America's Schools*. Online: http://mckinseyonsociety.com/downloads/reports/Education/achievement_gap_report.pdf (accessed on 13 October 2011).

Mediratta, K., Shah, S. and McAlister, S. (2008) *Organized Communities, Stronger Schools: A preview of research findings*. New York: Annenberg Institute for School Reform at Brown University.

Midwinter, E. (1972) *Priority Education: An account of the Liverpool Project*. Harmondsworth: Penguin.

Midwinter, E. (1973) *Patterns of Community Education*. London: Ward Lock.

Miller, R. (2008) *Education and Economic Growth: From the 19th to the 21st Century*, Cisco White Paper of Education and Economic Growth. Online: http://www.rielmiller.com/images/Education-and-Economic-Growth.pdf (accessed on 14 July 2010).

Ministry of Education (1944)'The Principles of Government in Maintained Secondary Schools', Cmd. 6523 (1944) followed by 'Administrative Memorandum, No. 25,' January (1945), quoted in Owen, J. (1978) *A New Partnership for Our Schools: The Taylor Report'*, *Oxford Review of Education*, 4(1): 4.

-- (1951), *Education 1900–1950*, Cmnd. 8244. London: HMSO.

Mongon, D. (2010) *The 2009 Inspection Framework: Well-being and community cohesion*. Nottingham: National College. Online: http://www.nationalcollege.org.uk/docinfo?id=132924&filename=inspection-framework-2009.pdf (accessed 19 September 2011).

Mongon, D., Allen, T., Farmer, L., and Atherton, C. (2010), *Emerging Patterns of Leadership: Co-location, Continuity, and Community*. Nottingham: National College.

Mongon, D. and Chapman, C. (2008) *Successful Leadership for Promoting the Achievement of White Working Class Pupils*. Nottingham: National College.

-- (2009) *Emerging Patterns of School Leadership: ECM perspectives.* Nottingham: National College for School Leadership. Online: http://www.nationalcollege. org.uk/docinfo?id=23805&filename=emerging-patterns-school-leadership-ecm-perspective.pdf (accessed 6 December 2011).

-- (2012) *High Leverage Leadership: Improving outcomes in educational settings.* London: Routledge.

Moore, M.H. (1995) *Creating Public Value Strategic Management in Government.* Cambridge, MA: Harvard University Press.

Morris, H. (1925) *The Village College. Being a Memorandum on the Provision of Educations and Social Facilities for the Countryside, with Special Reference to Cambridgeshire* (Section XIV). Online: http://www.infed.org/thinkers/et-morr. htm (accessed 3 June 2011).

NCSL (2009) *School Leadership Today.* Nottingham: The National College for Leadership of Schools and Children's Services. Online: http://www1. nationalcollege.org.uk/download?id=21843 (accessed 10 June 2011).

-- (2001) *Leadership Development Framework.* Nottingham: National College for School Leadership.

-- (2010) *What are new models and partnerships?* Nottingham: The National College for Leadership of Schools and Children's Services (now the National College for School Leadership). Online: http://www.nationalcollege.org.uk/ index/leadershiplibrary/leadingschools/modelsandpartnerships/what-are-new-models-of-leadership.htm (accessed on 16 May 2011).

Nooteboom, B. (2000) *Learning and Innovation in Organisations and Economies.* Oxford: Oxford University Press.

OECD (2001) *The Well-being of Nations: The role of human and social capital, education and skills.* Paris: Centre for Educational Research and Innovation OECD.

-- (2006) *Measuring the Effects of Education on Health and Civic Engagement,* Proceedings of the Copenhagen Symposium. Paris: OECD. Online: http:// www.oecd.org/dataoecd/23/61/37437718.pdf (accessed on 29 September 2011).

-- (2010a) *The High Cost of Low Educational Performance: The long-run economic impact of improving PISA outcomes.* Paris: OECD.

-- (2010b) *Improving Health and Social Cohesion through Education.* Paris:OECD. Online: http://www.keepeek.com/Digital-Asset-Management/ oecd/education/improving-health-and-social-cohesion-through-education_9789264086319-en (accessed on 29 September 2011).

-- (2010c) *What are the Social Benefits of Education?* Paris: OECD. Online: http://www.oecd-library.org/docserver/download/fulltext/9610061ec020.pdf?expires=1316088351andid=idandaccname=guestandchecksum=550293324E88F6F4154F86977771BF69 (accessed on 14 September 2011).

-- (2010d) *Ten Steps to Equity in Education.* Paris: OECD. Online: http://www.oecd.org/dataoecd/21/45/39989494.pdf (accessed on 30 September 2011).

-- (2011a) *Evaluation and Assessment Frameworks for Improving School Outcomes: Common policy challenges.* Paris: OECD. Online: http://www.oecd.org/edu/evaluationpolicy (accessed on 28 September 2011).

-- (2011b) *Society at a Glance 2011: OECD social indicators.* Paris: OECD. Online: http://www.oecd.org/document/24/0,3746,en_2649_37419_2671576_1_1_1_37419,00.html (accessed on 29 September 2011).

Ofsted (2002) *Teaching Assistants in Primary Schools: An evaluation of the quality and impact of their work.* London: Ofsted.

-- (2009) *The Annual Report of Her Majesty's Chief Inspector of Education, Children's Services and Skills 2008/09.* London: Ofsted.

-- (2010a) *The Annual Report of Her Majesty's Chief Inspector of Education, Children's Services and Skills 2009/10.* London: Ofsted. Online: http://www.ofsted.gov.uk/resources/annual-report-of-her-majestys-chief-inspector-of-education-childrens-services-and-skills-200910 (accessed on 21 September 2011).

-- (2010b) *School Governance: Learning from the best.* London: Ofsted.

O'Mara, A., Jamal, F., Llewellyn, A., Lehmann, A., Cooper, C. and Bergeron, C. (2010) *Improving Children's and Young People's Outcomes through Support for Mothers, Fathers, and Carers.* London: C4EO. Online: http://www.c4eo.org.uk/themes/families/effectivesupport/files/effective_support_research_review.pdf (accessed on 28 October 2011).

PAC (2009) *Widening Participation in Higher Education, House of Commons Public Accounts Committee, Fourth Report of Session 2008–09, HCC 226.* London: House of Commons. Online: http://www.publications.parliament.uk/pa/cm200809/cmselect/cmpubacc/226/9780215526557.pdf (accessed on 14 September 2011).

Payne, M. and Shand, R. (2009) adapted from Payne, C. and Scott, T. (1982) *Developing Supervision of Teams in Field and Residential Social Work.* London: National Institute of Social Work, Paper No 12.

Phillips, D. and Walford, G. (2006) *Tracing Education Policy: Selections from the Oxford Review of Education.* Abingdon: Routledge.

Plowden, B. (1967) *Children and their Primary Schools: A report of the Central Advisory Council for Education* (England). London: HMSO.

Punter, A. and Adams, J. (undated) *Looking after the governor is the business now*. Hatfield: University of Hertfordshire. Online: https://uhra.herts.ac.uk/dspace/bitstream/2299/862/1/102826.pdf (accessed on 27 September 2011).

PWC (2007) *Independent Study into School Leadership*, DCSF Research Report RR818A, DCSF-RW005. London: PricewaterhouseCoopers.

RAISE (2011) RAISEonline. Online: https://www.raiseonline.org/About.aspx (accessed 28 September 2011).

Richardson, W. and Wiborg, S. (2010) *English Technical and Vocational Education in Historical and Comparative Perspective*. London: Baker Dearing. Online: http://www.edge.co.uk/media/16991/considerations_for_university_technical_colleges.pdf (accessed on 14 September 2011).

Riddell, C.W. (2006) *The Impact of Education on Economic and Social Outcomes*. Vancouver: Department of Economics, University of British Columbia. Online: http://www.terry.uga.edu/~selgin/documents/impactofeducation.pdf (accessed on 28 September 2011).

Robinson, W. (2003) *Pupil Teachers and their Professional Training in Pupil Teacher Centres 1870–1914*. Lampeter: Edwin Mellen Press.

Robinson, V., Hohepa, M. and Lloyd, C. (2009) *School Leadership and Student Outcomes: Identifying what works and why – best evidence synthesis iteration*. Wellington: New Zealand Ministry of Education.

Russell, J. (2009) To unlock millions of children's lives, Britain must look to the Harlem miracle, *The Guardian*, 5 August. Online: http://www.guardian.co.uk/commentisfree/2009/aug/05/harlem-poverty-children-schools (accessed on 4 October 2011).

Smith, G., Smith, T. and Smith, T. (2007) Whatever Happened to EPAs? Part 2: Priority Areas – 40 years on. *FORUM*, Vol. 49, Numbers 1 & 2, 2007 141–56.

Southworth, G. (2004) *Primary School Leadership in Context: Leading small, medium and large sized schools*. London: RoutledgeFalmer.

Statham, J., Harris, A., Glenn, M., Morris, M., Marshall, H., Bergeron, C. and White, K. (2010) *Strengthening Family Wellbeing and Community Cohesion Through the Role of Schools and Extended Services*. London: Institute of Education, University of London.

Strand, S. (2008) *Minority Ethnic Pupils in the Longitudinal Study of Young People in England (LSYPE)*. London: DCSF. DCSF-RR029. Online: http://

www.dcsf.gov.uk/research/data/uploadfiles/DCSF-RR029.pdf (accessed 8 December 2009).

-- (2009) Race, sex, class and educational attainment: The case of white working class pupils. Paper presented to the Annual Conference of the British Educational Research Association, University of Manchester, Manchester, 2–5 September 2009.

Streatfield, D. and Jefferies, G. (1989) *Reconstitution of Governing Bodies: Survey 2*. Slough: NFER.

Szreter, S. (2004) The state of social capital: Bringing back in power, politics, and history. *Theory and Society*, 31(5), 573–621.

Talbot, C. (2009) Crafting public value, public governance, *Journal for Public Management* Autumn, 6–10.

Taylor, M. (2008) *Transforming Disadvantaged Places: Effective strategies for places and people*.York: Joseph Rowntree Foundation. Online: http://www.jrf.org.uk/publications/transforming-disadvantaged-places-effective-strategies-places-and-people (accessed 27 September 2011).

TDA (2010) *Parent Support Advisers: Practice and impact*. Manchester: TDA.

TGAT (1988) *National Curriculum Task Group on Assessment and Testing: A report*. London: DES.

Tomlinson, S. (2000) Ethnic minorities and education: New disadvantages, in Cox, T. (ed.) *Combating Educational Disadvantage: Meeting the needs of vulnerable children*. London: Routledge.

Total Place (2010) *Total Place: Better for Less*. Online: http://www.localleadership.gov.uk/totalplace/ (accessed 15 September 2011).

Treasury (2011) *Public Expenditure Statistical Analysis*. London: Treasury. Online: http://www.hm-treasury.gov.uk/pesa2011_section3.htm (accessed 9 September 2011).

UNESCO (2010) *EFA Global Monitoring Report: Reaching the marginalized*. Paris: UNESCO/Oxford University Press.

Välijärvi, J., Kupari, P., Linnakylä, P., Reinikainen, P., Sulkunen, S., Törnroos, J. and Arffman, I. (2007) *The Finnish success in PISA and some reasons behind it. PISA 2003*. Finnish Institute of Educational Research, University of Jyväskylä.

Walker, D. (2009) A stormy ride ahead for public value, public governance. *Journal for Public Management,* Autumn, 4–5.

Wallis, J. and Gregory, R. (2009) Leadership, accountability and public value: Resolving a problem in 'new governance'. *International Journal of Public Administration*, 32, 3–4, 250–73.

Ward, S. and Eden, C. (2009) *Key Issues in Education Policy*. London: Sage.

Warren, M. (2005) Communities and schools: A new view of urban school reform. *Harvard Educational Review*, 75(2) 133–173.

Watkins, C., Carnell, E. and Lodge, C. (2007) *Effective Learning in Classrooms*. London: Paul Chapman.

Whelan, F. (2009) *Lessons Learned: How good policies produce better schools*. London: MPG Books.

Whitty, G., Power, S. and Halpin, D. (1998) *Devolution and Choice in Education: The school, the state and the market*. Buckingham: Open University Press.

Wilkin, A., Kinder, K., White, R., Atkinson, M. and Doherty, P. (2003) *Towards the Development of 'Extended' Schools* (DfES Research Report 408). London: NFER.

Wilkin, A., Lamont, E., White, R., Kinder, K. and Howard, P. (2007) *Intervention Study: Schools as community based organisations*. London: CfBT. Online: http://www.cfbt.com/evidenceforeducation/our_research/evidence_for_schools/school_buildings/schools__the_community.aspx (accessed 27 September 2011).